Cheers fo
SEVEN Sɪ... ... ...

"*Sereni-Tea: Seven Sips to BLISS* is a leading-edge concept whose time has come! At a time when the world is making it harder to find a 'spot' of serenity, Dharlene Marie guides us towards inner peace, self-love and bliss, with a 'spot' of tea. Her gift is in making us pause to reflect upon and appreciate the richness of the tapestry we each have inside our hearts. This book is one fabulous gift that you should give to yourself and to those you love!" **Carole Lieberman, M.D.—Beverly Hills Psychiatrist, Best-selling Author and Talk Show Host— www.drcarole.com**

"The quest for success seems to be an ongoing struggle throughout our society. Dharlene Marie Fahl touches on the core issues of why success seems to elude so many people, and what simple and effective steps can to be taken to ensure it. *Sereni-Tea* is a "must read" in order to find out. It's well worth your time." **Michael Peak—Emmy Award Winning Television Journalist, Speaker and Seminar Producer**

"During times that are perceived as troubled or difficult, the greatest defense we have for a recession is going within. In *Sereni-Tea,* Dharlene Marie shows you how the recesses of your heart and mind will reward you with the purest and richest sense of inner peace and security; for therein lay all your true and infinite resources. Isn't it worth taking a sip or two, or seven, to find out? You will enjoy this book—the answers you seek are within." **September Dohrmann—Vice President & Treasurer—CEO Space**

"Dharlene Marie understands tea—in a way that most North Americans perhaps do not. I support her message of tea being a vehicle to bridge cultures and traditions, and equally so as a method for finding inner peace. As the daughter of a Japanese mother, I have a deep appreciation for the ceremony of tea and the detail, beauty and grace it entails; as a personal development and executive coach, I am passionate about supporting people to claim their power and find their center, which begins with mindfulness. Pour yourself a cup of tea and enjoy *Sereni-Tea,* that's an easy first step." **Denise Yamada—Emmy Award Winning Broadcast Journalist and Professional Certified Coach—www.DeniseYamada.com**

"The power of our every thought determines our choices and shapes our lives. *Sereni-Tea,* takes you through a gentle process to center your life while simply sipping a daily cup of tea. This book is a catalyst for positive change and an inspirational guide to having more peace with your mind, body, and soul. You will be touched by Dharlene Marie's gift of words as you journey into your own heart. Profoundly rich! Read this book to nurture your heart—and gift it to those whom you love!" **Sheryl Roush—Author of Heart of a Woman Book Series, Founder—Sparkle-Tudes!™—www.sparklepresentations. com**

"My pride is to have been one of the spiritual midwives who watched the birth of Dharlene Marie's vision. You could literally and metaphorically see that God was steeping this endeavor into something that would have the power to transform and heal. Let the power of her words fill your being; and all the better to do so with a lovely cup of tea. While your tea steeps into its perfection, pause and reflect on your own perfection. Taking time to sip and savor the tea allows you to absorb the power and potential of her guided meditation, each prayer, and the affirmations in *Sereni-Tea: Seven Sips to BLISS*. I know you will find exactly what you desire by loving and honoring yourself in this gentle and gracious experience of celebrating your true loving nature." **Reverend Duchess Dale—Spiritual Director, Chico New Thought Center for Spiritual Living in Chico, CA—www. chiconewthought.org**

"From one side of the globe to the other, from India to America, a love and fascination for tea has introduced Dharlene Marie Fahl to me and to the humanity of tea. Two seemingly different worlds can easily be united over tea. I see that her passion is to help you unite your outer world and your inner world. She helps you to do so here in *Sereni-Tea* while sipping a cup of tea. As there is turmoil in our outer world, many are faced with inner turmoil, as well. In seven sips of tea, Ms. Fahl (we call her Marie in India) shows you how easily and effortlessly you can end your own inner conflict." **Rajiv Lochan, Siliguir, India—Founder of Lochan Tea—Owner Doke Tea Estate—www.lochantea. com www.doketea.in**

"As you wrap your hands around a soothing cup of tea you are embracing so much more. Life is about love, light and the luxury of taking time for yourself. In as little as seven sips of tea you can easily and joyfully find yourself in a place of bliss, Dharlene Marie shows you just how do this in her book, *Sereni-Tea.* Go ahead and try it—give yourself an enlightening tea experience." **James Pham—CEO/Founder—EnlighTea Cafes—www. enlightea.com**

"Discovering your own personal power is the key to success in all areas of life, and while sipping a cup of tea, Dharlene Marie Fahl guides you to a place of serenity where you can access your personal power—your mind. Each sip of tea allows you to calm your mind and be at peace with your thoughts, and along with an open heart you will surely find your bliss and be on your way to living a powerful life. Make this a goal for yourself—give yourself the gift of blissfully mastering your mind and you can start by reading *Sereni-Tea: Seven Sips to BLISS.*" **William T. Hultquist—CEO—Master Mind to Personal Power Mentor—www.mmtpp.com**

"Soothe your spirit, calm your mind, tea isn't just for drinking anymore. Dharlene Marie shows you how you can soothe and calm yourself while sipping and savoring tea. She is right, in seven sips of tea you can easily be on your way to bliss—the natural way. I know you will truly enjoy discovering this process as you sip tea and read her book, *Sereni-Tea,* **Stephanie Ringgold— Founder—RoyalMajesTea—www.royalmajestea.com**

"As an instructor of the Japanese Tea Ceremony in Fukuroi Shi, Shizuoka, Japan, and translator of American and Japanese tea books, I know of the wonders of tea. I have also seen how tea is uniting many from around the world. Marie-san, as we call her in Japan, came to my country and made instant friends with so many. We are supporting her with her books about tea and serenity and helping others appreciate tea. Please enjoy her book, *Sereni-Tea*: *Seven Sips to BLISS.*" **Ako Yoshino—English Instructor, University of Shizuoka, Tea Ceremony Instructor, Translator—http://www.geocities.jp/nihonsadojuku/tusin. htm**

"Being a firm believer that whatever we put into our bodies' impacts us greatly, I am totally with Dharlene Marie Fahl as she says here in*, Sereni-Tea,* whatever we *think*, and the emotion behind each thought, impact us just as much. We both agree wholeheartedly that tea is one of the best things we can do for our minds, our bodies and our souls. As the author of, *"The Ultimate Tea Diet"* and tea expert, I know how empowering moments with a cup of tea can be for the psyche and the body as well. Life is all about balance: creating it, allowing it, surrendering to it, and even finding it in a cup of tea. I know you will enjoy this book. Keep sipping—bliss is there." **Mark "dr. tea" Ukra**

"In promoting 'tea excellence' there are many aspects to consider in producing and serving an excellent cup of tea—far too many for you as a reader to concern yourself with. It is my hope and sincere desire that while reading, *Sereni-Tea* by Dharlene Marie, you will be sipping many cups of excellent tea. If you are enjoying the tea—then it is excellent and that is what matters. We do want the world to experience more tea and more bliss." **Kaushik Bhattacharjee—Assistant Director—Darjeeling Tea Research & Management Association, India—www. nitm.in**

In all my years of drinking and sharing tea, I have seen it put to use in so many wonderful ways. In *Sereni-Tea*: *Seven Sips to BLISS*, Dharlene Marie takes you on a journey beyond simply enjoying the beverage, teaching you how tea can help you discover yourself. Each sip does indeed have the power to take you on a voyage of self-reflection and helps to nurture self-love and spiritual growth. Success, love and bliss will be different for each and every one of us—but ALL of us deserve them. Take your time and enjoy this book." **Jane Pettigrew—Author, International Tea Consultant and Trainer**

"Dharlene Marie is motivational in promoting health and well being. Her advocacy for teens and their long term health goes unmatched. Her writings here in *Sereni-Tea* will inspire your soul, warm your heart and stimulate your mind. Enjoy your moments of peace, your moments of reflection, and above all, the golden delight, we call, tea." **Kristina Wiley, DDS— Founder—Linde Lane Teas, LLC**

"Stress is a major culprit in our current society which is leading us to some serious health challenges. In *Sereni-Tea* Dharlene Marie shows us some very simple techniques that indeed help to reduce and relieve our modern stress levels. You will certainly feel better for having read this book—buy a copy for someone you love who needs it!" **Roy John Robinson D.C., M.D.— Weight Loss Specialist**

"Dharlene Marie Fahl has skillfully melded three of her passions into one vehicle, *Sereni-Tea*; her love of tea, her love of poetry and her love of helping others. Her presentations to our Meetup group were very well received." **Dianna Harbin—Certified Tea Professional (STI)—Founder of San Diego Tea Meetup.**

Sereni-Tea

SEVEN SIPS TO BLISS

Dharlene Marie Fahl

Transformation Media Books
Bloomington, Indiana, U.S.A. 2009

Transformation Media Books

Published by Transformation Media Books, USA
www.TransformationMediaBooks.com

An imprint of Pen & Publish, Inc.
Bloomington, Indiana
(812) 837-9226
info@PenandPublish.com

www.PenandPublish.com

Copyright © 2012 Dharlene Marie Fahl

Special Credits

Personal photo: Rachel Wattson Photography
Cover Design: Min Gates - MinDesigns
Final Edits: Trish Brown, Tyler Sparks

ISBN: 978-0-9844600-3-8
Library of Congress Control Number: 20109928449

This book is printed on acid free paper.

Printed in the USA

Sereni-Tea

In peaceful repose, I breathe in all that I am.
I marvel at the simplicity and purity of divine serenity.
From this place of perfection I am undisturbed.
I am calm and refreshed, most unperturbed.
I see God, I feel God, I hear the word.
Clearly and calmly, I am one with this Force.
I am intact; I am whole, pure and good.
I see the reflection of my own perfection; no defects
and no deficiencies.
Nothing can diminish the goodness
and the God-ness of me.
In serenity and with deep gratitude,
and along with each sip of tea
I realize God is all of me from within me.
And this is my place of bliss—
from here I can do and be anything.
So with ease and grace I surrender my pace.
I have nothing to fear; there is no race.
No rush, no hurry, no finish line.
Every day I know victory in the arms of the Divine;
my giver, my deliverer, the provider of bliss.
I need for nothing; the aches are all gone.
My soul is free to be all that it is—love is all it can be,
and that's good enough for me.
Amen.

Dedication

To all the tea drinkers and to the seekers and followers of bliss:
May each of you find the inner peace of self-love while
"taking up the cup."

For those with an established affinity for tea:
This is the cup of kindness,
and it is meant to be shared.
After you have sipped it for yourself,
please pass it along.

Table of Contents

"If you do follow your bliss you put yourself on a kind of track that has been there all the while, waiting for you, and the life that you ought to be living is the one you are living. Follow your bliss and don't be afraid, and doors will open where you didn't know they were going to be."

~ Joseph Campbell ~

Foreword

Yes, indeed there is bliss to be found in a cup of tea! As fellow tea colleagues, Dharlene Marie Fahl and I understand tea in very similar ways. We have both been blessed with the opportunity to travel to many places in the world and have seen firsthand the magic of tea and tea people. In the world of tea there are no strangers, only friends with whom we have not yet sipped. Tea sippers are joined in a common, perhaps intrinsic union; symbiotic, similar to the leaf and the land. The spirit of tea resonates with the vibrations of humanity and this interplay is captured in Dharlene Marie's seven sip process—inner peace leads to a more peaceful 'outer' world.

As a martial arts practitioner of 30 years, I have learned the value of a peaceful mind. As founder of The Tea House and World Tea Tours, I have seen cultural and language barriers disappear over the simple sharing of a cup of tea. I have been invited into tea fields and factories around the world including places which are seldom privy to outsiders—doors opened by a mutual love and appreciation for the tea leaf.

Dharlene Marie and I shared the stage at the first Indian Tea Forum in Siliguri, India in 2010, where once again we were blessed to witness parts of the world coming together over tea.

Tea is definitely a beverage that leads one to the doors 'inside.' Upon crossing the threshold and entering into the garden of bliss—a place that has no boundaries, borders, or barriers— anything can manifest in your life.

If tea is a new beverage to you then it is my privilege to welcome you into a world of profound realization; a galaxy of serenity and tranquility. There is so much more in your cup than simply a liquid. In a way, it contains the elixir of humanity. The mystery of the tea leaf and the magic of the tea infusion have been captivating mankind for thousands of years—I invite you to now join us.

For those of you well acquainted with tea, do yourself the favor of taking these seven sips to bliss and having a full and total experience of this ancient and alluring beverage known the world over as, TEA.

Dan Robertson
Naperville, Illinois
Founder of The Tea House,
World Tea Tours and the
International Tea Cuppers Club
www.theteahouse.com
www.worldteatours.com
www.teacuppers.com

Acknowledgements

As we walk our path in life we are blessed by those who join us; some for awhile, and others, forever, even if it is only in spirit.

The love and spirit of my two children, David-Alexander and Savannah, will be with me forever. I am blessed that you both chose me to be your mother. The energy of your maturing teen spirits keeps me young and vital and strong enough to handle anything. Thank you, you are the best, and I love you both.

To the twelve people in the Foundational Class of 2003 at Pacific Church of Religious Science, along with Reverend Duchess Dale, where my whole tea journey began and I became a writer, I cannot say thank you enough.

For all my fellow tea aficionados and colleagues in the industry, as you all share your love and fascination for this beverage, the world becomes a gentler place as individuals are finding and sipping their bliss.

To my fellow alumni of Mark Victor Hansen's Inner Circle, we are still movers and shakers and we *will* change the world as Mark has taught us. May the circle continue to grow and the ripples be felt all over the world.

To Stan and Callie Spilman, my earth angels, I will be forever grateful for the kindness you have shown to me and my children.

Mr. Wynn, what could be is never as powerful as what is. Thank you for what is.

Affirmation

All that I have learned about myself,
I can now accept.
I choose love and respect,
and reject anything less.

Bliss

What is it that we are all looking for? Why are we walking around in a daze of self-denial and self-depletion? How do we fill up that hole inside of us that keeps telling us we need more? When will we find happiness? Where do we even look for happiness or joy?

This is an instant gratification society and we are all being led and mislead moment-to-moment by every media source that we have access to.

Joy and bliss—what on earth are they? Will we ever find them here on earth? They sound like something one can only experience in Heaven.

In our North American culture we want it all and we believe we are entitled to it all, as well, and we want it NOW! We are busy people. We have goals, we have aspirations and we are all out there doing our best to be "successful" and we will do whatever it takes to achieve success. Yet most of us are almost as clued out about success as we are about bliss.

We think success is the vehicle we drive, the house we live in, the schools we went to or are sending our kids to. We believe it is tied into how much our salary is, how many initials are behind our name, the person on our arm, the view from our home and office, or the credit score some institution gave us. Success seems measurable. How many stories have we heard, though, about "successful" people who were found face down on the floor in their homes dead from a drug overdose or something similar? Why weren't they happy? They appeared to have it all—why hadn't they found their bliss?

Bliss comes from within—always has and always will. You will never find it in a bottle, in chocolate cake, in a pill, from a person, on a remote mountain top, in a new city or country, with a new lover, when you have a specific dollar amount in the bank, or when the kids have finished college.

Bliss is what excites your soul and delights your heart. Bliss is whatever you can do for hours that seem to go by like only minutes—when you totally lose track of time because you are so fulfilled. When, and if we use the terms *joy* and *bliss,* they seem to be rather elusive—but only because we use them so infrequently—it is happiness and success we appear to be striving for because those bring instant gratification, and those things we do recognize.

Do we always know when we are happy and successful? It rarely seems like it is enough, though, that there could always be more, that we could certainly have more.

Therein lays the difference and the explanation of bliss. Yes, we do use the term "blissed-out" but that is generally an incorrect usage of the word because it is usually some outside or foreign substance that causes us to be blissed-out.

Bliss presents itself in quiet moments and this is why I believe with just seven sips of tea, in tender and tranquil moments of total surrender and serenity, you will get a taste of bliss; a sensation of bliss, and yes, perhaps even feeling blissed-out; naturally.

So many are asking, "What is my purpose?" "What am I here to do?" What is my destiny?" People are asking these, as well as numerous other questions incredibly similar. Pour yourself a cup of tea, get quiet, take seven slow sips, and then ask those questions. Ask with a clear mind, an open heart and a sincere desire to receive the answers. Finding your bliss is doing whatever makes you truly happy. Following your bliss is doing it—all the time!

Bliss comes when you stop hating yourself—when you stop picking apart everything you have ever done or have not yet accomplished. Bliss can only present itself when you are loving yourself. A mind full of criticism, self-doubt and self-loathing is not the home of bliss. A heart that has shut down and knows not forgiveness isn't a dwelling place for bliss.

Get yourself ready for your bliss. Sit down with a cup of tea and start the process of releasing all those limiting, small thoughts you ever had about yourself. When you can get yourself to a place of loving and accepting yourself—just as you are RIGHT NOW—you will find your bliss.

To follow your bliss is to follow your heart. It is to be strong and courageous enough to do the things you love to do—even if they do not bring you the monetary benefits others will say you need in order to survive. The goal with bliss is not survival—it is 'thrival.' When you are thriving—anything is possible.

Finding your bliss can involve other people, however, it is about getting 'right' with yourself first, then moving forward to love others and assist others. Getting and receiving bliss is reciprocal but it starts with you. Discover what makes you happy—decide to do more of that—determine who else could benefit from the fruits of your bliss—then do it!

Take those precious and life-sustaining moments with a cup of tea to ask your higher self to help you in answering your questions. Stay awake and alert and you will be presented with the answers. I call this 'sipping your bliss.'

In the fifteen or so, mindful minutes it takes to sip a cup of tea seven times, you can begin to change your life, or perhaps to simply enhance it. Bliss is about loving yourself. Can you take the time daily—15 minutes—to love yourself and find your bliss?

Loving yourself is the greatest success you will ever know.

I can almost guarantee you that every decision you have ever made in life, whether it was a business choice, the starting or ending of a relationship, financial or personal, small or huge; was based on how much you loved yourself or didn't love yourself at the time of making that decision.

It is now time to find your bliss and make empowered life choices for yourself. Your bliss will lead you down a path of fulfillment and should life ever get the better of you—even for a few moments—sit down with a cup of tea and in seven sips claim it back!

Seven Sips to Bliss

A Guided Meditation

We are sensual beings, we are sentient beings, we are magnificent spiritual beings, and yes, we are human beings. Do not let that last one bring you down for within the human body, mind, and heart, there is a soul, and this soul makes you infinite. How do we access this soul—this 'spiritual' aspect of ourselves? In seven sips I will show you how. No, we will not be sipping some concoction with hallucinogenic qualities, we will be sipping, TEA. Are you asking to yourself, "What, plain old, boring old tea?" In the chapters ahead I will dispel the myth that tea can or could ever be plain old boring. Oh, certainly not. Right now, with each of the seven sips of tea, I wish to reunite you with something you were born with but somehow lost along the way. I am choosing *not* to call them 'steps,' they are seven *sips* to bliss.

We are sensual beings blessed with physical senses—modalities for experiencing everything around us—endowments we have taken for granted—gifts we have shut down or have never truly utilized consciously. I am not speaking of anything sexual; sensual and sensuous are not necessarily sexual in context. I am referring to actively engaging all of our physical senses and accessing our own personal power in order to raise our vibratory levels to where we begin to feel and find our bliss.

As sentient beings we are so much more than we have been taught to believe we are. Something greater is always going on behind the scenes and even right in front of our eyes. When we are able to break the trance we've been living in and raise our consciousness, our sentient powers will emerge. We can do this by gaining mastery over our "monkey minds"—by taking control of negative and demeaning thoughts and replacing them with positive and uplifting thoughts that have *feelings* attached to them.

As human beings we are confined physically within a human body; or are we? Being spiritual in nature surely we can break free of those confines and certainly we can have peace of mind while still alive in this human body. The precincts and prisons exist in our minds and in seven sips—let's see if we can break free.

Please prepare yourself a cup of tea and sit up straight in a chair with a full back support next to a table on which to place your cup.

SIP ONE

Wrap your hands gently around the cup of tea; if it is too hot simply hold your hands very near the sides of the cup—look at the contents of the cup—see the colour and clarity—peer all the way down to the bottom of the cup—then look beyond the bottom.

Tap very lightly the sides of the cup—several times—feel the sparks—feel the heat of the cup in all of your fingers—allow the tender and tingling sensation of the warmth to travel up your arms and flow freely into your entire body.

Taking the handle—bring the cup close to your nose—breathe in the aroma—breathe in and out three times—gradually and evenly.

Take the cup to your lips, if it is very hot, sip slightly and slowly—swallow and bring this liquid into your body.

SIP TWO

Feel your shoulders relaxing—your neck loosening—forehead expanding—your heart slowing down—your lower body getting heavier and heavier; you are letting go. Allow yourself to enjoy this experience—free of expectation and free of inhibition. Take another sip—feel the tea on your tongue and on the sides of your cheeks—swallow slowly. You are totally safe and comfortable—tension begins to escape from your mind and body with each breath you take.

SIP THREE

Let out a long, slow sigh of relief. Take another sip, swallow and sigh deeply once more. Allow whatever thoughts that come into your head to simply move on. Nothing to think about—nothing to worry about—let go completely. Something marvelous is happening. Feel your heart expanding—each breath enlarges this area. See it growing in your mind—bringing full attention to your heart. Send it love—feel it responding. Touch your heart area with your right hand—your hand is warm from holding the cup—feel that sensation—take in that warmth—feel the love. This is you—loving yourself.

SIP FOUR

Feeling completely relaxed and totally at ease—bring the cup to your lips and sip. You are alert and conscious and completely content. Stress has released its hold on you—your mind is quiet—surrender again as you swallow. Continue to breathe with your heart. Bring your awareness now to a happy memory: the birth of a child, your wedding day, your graduation day, hearing the words, "I love you" being whispered in your ear, stroking a sleeping pet, jumping for joy, the smile of a child or a complete stranger, pride in a job well done, an infant gripping your finger. There are so many. Remember how you felt on that occasion and allow yourself to feel those feelings again. Stay with those sensations of well being. You are doing a great job at taking yourself to another state of consciousness; another state of awareness.

SIP FIVE

Both hands are still holding the cup—it has cooled down significantly—the delightful aroma lingers—your taste buds are entirely alive and anticipating this next sip. All your senses are fully heightened and you feel totally exhilarated and peaceful at the same time. Look into your cup as you sip. Invite your soul to make its presence known—swallow—remain very calm and tranquil while still holding all your pleasant memories at the forefront of your mind and in your heart—*smile*. Know that your life matters. Feel gratitude and appreciation for the magnificence of YOU; yes, you and your very valid place in this world.

SIP SIX

Scan your body slowly from your toes up to the top of your head—invite your soul to scan it with you. Feel it entering every cell of your body, every organ, every muscle, every element of your physical being. Take another sip. Your soul is in that sip, too, and has entered your body from your lips and nostrils—into your stomach and lungs—breathe it throughout your entire being—and beyond. Trust that it knows what to do—trust that it knows very well the way to your heart. Feel the congruency and your oneness with all that is. Say out loud, a breath-filled, 'thank you.'

SIP SEVEN

Let sip seven take you to Heaven—whatever your version or vision of it might be—go there in your mind. Hold the tea in your mouth as you are propelled on an inward and upward journey. Feel who you are coming back together—heart, head, body and soul all as one—aligned with something far greater than yourself. Swallow and take it all in. Rest in this place—for you have now successfully raised your own vibratory level and opened the door to your bliss. It was not locked, perhaps where you thought there were only walls, a door has appeared—enter—you are most welcome. What questions do you have to ask? Ask—and you will receive. Remember this place—you have been here before—long, long ago. Remember these feelings. Your bliss has been waiting for you—receive it. You have come home. Set the cup down and simply be—you have arrived.

~ ~ ~ ~ ~ ~ ~

Taking yourself from a place in your mind of chaos and confusion to a place of congruency and coherence can actually be scientifically measured—this is not all just "woo-woo, airy-fairy" stuff. The heart and mind together are incredibly powerful; as are people. Heart-based living reduces stress significantly and personal coherence leads to global coherence. Please check out the work that is being at The Institute of HeartMath www.heartmath.org

Most of us don't understand why we don't achieve our goals. We don't understand that our mind is bound and determined to lock us into permanent stagnation. If you are interested in freeing yourself from the self doubt that causes so much pain and procrastination and wish to learn how to recruit your mind into helping you achieve your goals—then please give yourself a gift and check out www.mastermindtopersonalpower.com or www.mmtpp.com

"You have work to do, and you wonder if you can manage it. You hesitate a little, then you make up your mind, and finally you succeed, you lift this weight ... you move that obstacle. This proves you are capable of such efforts, and in recognizing your possibilities; you feel your force and your faith grow. Faith, then, is linked to the assurance we gain through our triumphs. This law is borne all the more in the spiritual realm. From one effort to another, all your untried capabilities come out into the light of day and make themselves known. But you must be reasonable and begin modestly by accomplishing small things at first. So many people have been stopped in their evolution because they failed to begin modestly."

~ Omraam Mikhaël Aïvanhov ~

Introduction

It is always a blessing to be guided by the forces of the universe—here you are holding this book and perhaps wondering why. Something far greater than us is always at work and has led you here. In order to find your bliss there must be a surrendering to that *"something."*

Thank you for opening up to this three-part journey. Oh, you didn't know this was the beginning of a special journey? Ah, but you did, and this is the beauty of how our wonderful universe works. Here you are at the commencement of finding your bliss through a three-book series that I call, The Tea Trilogy. As a certified tea specialist, I write for the novice tea drinker and as an ordained minister, I write for the neophyte spiritual seeker. My goal is to bring the two together; to introduce tea drinkers to a spiritual practice that includes their beloved beverage, to acquaint the spiritual seeker with the ancient rituals and traditions of taking tea, and to be here with YOU on this inauguration, at the first sip you take toward finding your bliss. Bliss is the uniting of your inner world with your outer world.

This is where taking fifteen minutes to love yourself can easily begin. In the time it takes to mindfully sip a cup of tea—you can change your life. For some of you, it will be the beginning of your new life; others are well advanced and need only quiet moments for remembering. For everyone, though, it is a surrendering.

Turning tea drinking into something spiritual and sacred is not new, though it is certainly a match made in Heaven, and now you can have a little piece of Heaven with each sip of tea. If Heaven is not what you are seeking—you will still be able to take a taste of bliss, one sip at a time. It is my intention to get you started on the quest to bliss with book one of the Tea Trilogy, *Sereni-Tea: Seven Sips to BLISS*.

Tea is the number one beverage on the planet, next to water. It has a rich and well-steeped history in just about every country in this fabulous world of ours. That means there is a lot to learn about tea but in this book I will not overwhelm you; my intention is to delight you with just enough tea knowledge to whet your appetite for this intriguing beverage.

The Tea Trilogy is carefully laid out to take you on a three-step process of healing and self-discovery—the essential precursors to finding your bliss. Each book is created to stand alone so you will feel complete by the end of each journey and ready for the next adventure into yourself. When we begin anything new we usually have some old stuff to get rid of first, and most of that junk lives in our heads, in our thoughts. Book one, this book, goes right to the epicenter of the so-called problem area—the mind, the busy lower mind where the chatter never ceases and where we sabotage our own bliss.

This part of the mind is like taking a walk down the center aisle of a carnival with non-stop barkers accosting you from every angle. This book will aid you in creating a spiritual practice for yourself; quiet and special time you give yourself while having a cup of tea. Therefore, treating yourself to a perfect mind, body and soul experience in the time it takes to sip a cup of tea. You see, true bliss is a choice, and a gift you give yourself, not something someone else has to teach you.

Book Two—*Sancti-Tea* takes you into the heart for the healing of the wounds that still live there. It is a fiction, non-fiction combination where I take you around the world of tea and lead you into 13 fictional heart-opening journeys of healing where you are served tea in perhaps some of the most unlikely places by some mysterious and some familiar folks. A healed heart is an open heart; one ready to love and be loved fully. The journey from the mind to the heart need not be difficult or lengthy; it is indeed an expedition worth taking though, at any risk. The only things you will be in jeopardy of losing are fear, doubt and stagnation. Letting go of all three of these is what will lead you to a place of bliss—your place—one that you do indeed deserve.

Book Three—*Divini-Tea* leads you to a sacred place and allows you to create your own special and unique relationship with the Divine through prayer. Your mind will be at peace, your heart will be wide open, and you will know joy and bliss and be completely ready to taste the divinity and perfection of your own authentic self. To assist you on this journey of prayer I have written 101 healing prayers to enjoy with a cup of tea. I share these prayers with you throughout the three books; the final book contains the complete collection of all my healing tea prayers.

The Healing Prayers are written using universal principles of God. Some of the prayers are for releasing old, limiting thoughts and beliefs; others are to attract the people and things you would like in your life. Some are simply prayers of gratitude where you express your thanks for all God is, for all you have, and all you are right now. Every prayer is a celebration of bliss.

I say that I am a "spiritual seeker." As an ordained minister, I am "trans-denominational," one who chooses to transcend religion, as opposed to non-denominational. I have and will continue to ask a lot of questions about who we are, why we are here, where we came from, and of course, where we are going. But wouldn't it be nice to enjoy the journey all along the way? What seems to me to be the most significant question is—how can we live in joy and bliss as we are discovering ourselves?

"Ask and you will receive; seek and you will find, knock and the door will open unto you." These wise words were given to us over two thousand years ago. They give us permission to ask, and they allow us the freedom to seek and to knock on the door of bliss. And then, to have that door open wide as you cross the "Welcome" mat.

Even if we are not aware of it, we are all seeking something—I believe it is inner peace; a sense of contentment and a knowing that the universe is in divine right order—no matter how it may sometimes appear! We are seeking serenity and tranquility, which is not something we will find outside of ourselves—it lays waiting within each and every one of us and is how we access our own ability to achieve true bliss. With dedicated and quiet moments, sipping serenity is very simple. This is how the Truth is uncovered and discovered—with simplicity—and this is where you will discover that you are now on a spiritual journey. Sit down and pour yourself a cup of tea and see what happens—sit down and start loving yourself.

Spirituality is something we are all born *with* and something we just *allow* to happen naturally because it is innate. Religion, on the other hand, seems to be something we are born *into,* taught, and then expected to apply. Being in spirit or with spirit is part of our divine nature, it is who we are. To be inspired or "in spirit" comes as naturally as breathing (as the word actually implies) and the mere act of consciously drawing air into our lungs reconnects us with the entire universe.

What you will read in the pages ahead is what I believe to be true. Truths whispered to me in quiet times while sipping tea, truths I've read, truths I've studied, and truths I've tested, as well as tasted. Whatever does not feel "right" for you—simply discard—for this is your journey of bliss and you are the creator of your life and all that happens in your life.

Who else am I? I am the mother of two growing, entrepreneurial, free-spirited, free-thinking young adults, whose current and future well-being is still one of my main concerns. I am recently divorced after 20 years of marriage and still friends with my ex-husband, the father of my children for whose support and dedication I will always be extremely grateful. I am an aging baby boomer making healthier and wiser choices for my body temple. I am a writer and a poetess learning to use a voice I never claimed before, in a way I never dreamed possible. I am a former business owner and restaurateur, and will always be an entrepreneur. I am a daughter now finally able to understand the joys and woes of parenthood. I am a sister accepting that families do not happen randomly. I am a citizen with a new understanding of the teaching, "Love thy neighbor as thyself." I am a friend learning that listening is the greatest gift you can give someone. I am a school and church volunteer learning about service and community and humanity. I am a seeker choosing to open my eyes and see with my heart. And yes, I am still a Canadian after living in San Diego for 22 years, and I choose to still spell like one.

Most significantly though, I am a child of God, and that makes me just like you.

Being a seeker, I was fascinated to learn about tea and the spiritual significances this beverage has been associated with for thousands of years. The questions I asked about tea have led me across the world; they have introduced me to new customs and cultures and to some people that will be my friends for the rest of my life. I have walked the pristine tea fields in silence and listened to the whispers of the leaves. I now share my tea trips in TEA TALKS with many groups as I teach them about tea and have them taste teas from all over the world.

One day, over an extraordinary pot of oolong tea as I watched the tea leaves unfurl in the water, I saw them as a metaphor for life. Like me, like most of us, the leaves unfolded to reveal their treasures but only after a long process of cultivation, careful handling, and finally, total immersion in the hot water of life's experiences. As the tea leaves surrendered to the water, all their gifts were released. Just as we are learning to surrender to a Power and a Force beyond ourselves in order to just go with it and not against it. Therein, lays the true secret of bliss.

This evolving journey of life does indeed present challenges, and this book strives to address some of them, as well as to suggest how to begin a new journey toward the inner peace of bliss. I know firsthand how self-doubt, low self-esteem and the lack of self-love, as well as the trappings of a chaotic lower mind can lead to behaviours that end up being self-destructive and extremely limiting. My crutch along this pilgrimage has been food, and it started at a very early age for me. Twelve years ago, I dragged around a body with one hundred extra pounds. For the first time in my life, I have been able to have the experience of seeing my body weight, height, and age all in the same category on medical charts; never in my childhood or adolescent years did I have this experience. Oh, twenty pounds still come and go, but for the most part I have maintained the majority of that weight release for over a decade.

For years I sought almost every weight-loss method there was "out there," until I learned that what I needed was within me. I have lived through the agony of those dark days of shame, but now I *know* there is light—not just at the end of the tunnel when I reached a certain weight, but all through it, and I now know the light comes from *me*. These were truly moments of bliss.

It is my hope that in reading, **Sereni-Tea**: *Seven Sips to Bliss,* you will feel inspired to "take up the cup" and enjoy this wonderful beverage known and treasured for thousands of years, this mystical remedy called, "tea."

When you do yourself the kindness of giving tea a special place in your life, it becomes part of a spiritual practice—no matter what your religion is. It connects you to a sacred tradition, as well as to the many who have honoured it for millennia. By the simple act of preparing and drinking tea, you give yourself permission to be in charge of your own well-being and your own bliss.

When the cup is filled with kindness and shared with others, we will have successfully found our way back to unconditional love—for this is where we all come from and something we are all capable of when we surrender.

And yes, we are *beings*, spiritual beings in human form. We do not always have to be *doing.* Taking time for tea gives us back our purpose to simply *be.*

With each sip of *Sereni-Tea* you are taken deeper and closer to whatever your personal definition of bliss ends up being; just as you'll end up being all you were created to be. Namaste.

To your true BLISS—cheers!

Dharlene Marie Fahl

Affirmation

I sip to you.
I sip to me.
I sip to Sereni-Tea.

"The first cup moistens my lips and throat. The second cup breaks my loneliness. The third cup searches my barren entrails but to find therein some thousand volumes of odd ideographs. The fourth cup raises a slight perspiration—all the wrongs of life pass out through my pores. At the fifth cup I am purified. The sixth cup calls me to the realms of the immortals. The seventh cup—ah, but I could take no more! I only feel the breath of the cool wind that raises in my sleeves. Where is Elysium? Let me ride on this sweet breeze and waft away thither."

~ Lu Tung ~

Compatibili-Tea

Love has its season just as God has Its reason.
I stand steady as I allow my heart to get ready.
I am open to receive and I choose to believe God is all there is.
Love is all there is. One with God, one with all;
from the One Mind, I have one in mind;
a mate, a match, loveable and compatible.
First, I accept and love myself for the growing spirit I am.
Seeing my own good allows me to see
the congeniality of the right person for me.
In loving myself, pure love is what I attract;
this is a universal law—a divine fact.
I'll settle for nothing less. I claim my own happiness.
I send out thanks, I know I've been heard.
I trust divine timing and I trust the Word.
God's time is my time and I let it all be.
I choose love and acceptance.
I'll just wait and see.
I have faith on my side and with God
as my guide, true love will abide.
All is perfect for me.
Amen.

"I am so fond of tea that I could write a
whole dissertation on its virtues. It comforts and enlivens
without the risks attendant on spirituous liquors.
Gentle herb!
Let the florid grape yield to thee. Thy soft influence is a
more safe inspirer of social joy!"

~ James Boswell ~

Prosperi-Tea

Now is my time to flourish.
All the gifts of the kingdom are mine.
God knows only success, from now on, I choose nothing less.
God is all I know. God is all there is.
Our promising, auspicious selves are one.
All outcomes are propitious and prosperous.
I thrive in the contentment of this knowledge
and this brings me infallible courage.
My every endeavour yields only good;
because I claim all my good, all of my gifts.
Wealth and well-being go hand-in-hand;
giving is receiving, this I understand.
I accept this well-being and do well.
I give thanks and credit God, whose love
reveals my true unlimited potential.
I surrender all of my fears over to God.
Money is energy and I let it flow.
I release old beliefs—I simply let them go.
I attain and obtain all through God.
We grow and prosper as one.
I trust the Divine Wisdom, I seize the day
and God shows me the way.
Prosperity comes to me now.
Amen.

"Enjoy life sip by sip, not gulp by gulp."

~ Minister of Leaves ~

Ami-Tea

This is my prayer for peace and friendship,
for a world in divine harmony and kinship;
a world that knows no war.
To do this, I bring myself to a peaceful place.
I go within and know that
God is all there is and I am one with this divine tranquility.
I pray that everyone joins me in this sacred space of amity.
For this is the place where peace
begins—this powerful, productive and potent place within.
From here we see only our similarities and parity
and know only our good.
I accept good, embody good, live for good, and do only good.
As I know peace, I know it begins with me.
I give thanks and abide by the Golden Rule, the code of amity
and know no enemy.
I put aside and I go inside. I release and I relent.
I forgive and I repent. I let go and I let God.
I give in and I get God. And so it is, and so I am
and so we have peace.
Amen.

Affirmation

All that I am and all that I seek
dwells quietly and peacefully within me.

Chapter One

Tea Enlightenment

Affirmation

As I sip the tea,
I discover and uncover the real me.

Tea Enlightenment

TEA is an ancient beverage, believed to have been discovered in China well over 4,000 years ago. The legend goes that while the Emperor Shen Nung was boiling water outside on an open fire, some leaves from the Camellia sinensis plant blew into his pot. As he sipped the uplifting brew, he just knew there was something special about this evergreen bush.

Cultivation of the tea plant and use of its leaves spread throughout China and Japan mostly by Buddhist monks who used the leaves as a medicine. They also used this cha, as it is called in several languages, as a means for staying awake during long hours of meditation. In an effort to combat intemperance, the monks also offered tea as an alternative to alcoholic beverages.

It wasn't until early in the 17th century that the Dutch began importing tea from China. Thereafter, tea made its way from Holland to England and then to North America. Today, it is found all over the globe, where it is used in spiritual celebrations, meditations, cultural rituals and social functions. Tea has been used to enhance traditions, reflect customs, and bridge cultures. For some time now, tea has been the number two beverage in the world, second only to water.

All true TEA comes from the same plant. (The term "herbal tea" is misleading, because it is not technically *tea* but rather an infusion of the seeds, flowers, roots, bark, leaves and/or berries of various edible plants.) White tea, green tea, oolong and black tea all come from the Camellia sinensis, a subtropical evergreen tree. Skillful manipulation of the leaves determines the tea type. When the natural enzymes of the leaf are exposed to the air through a rolling process, the cell structure begins to break down. This is known as oxidation. The classification of the tea—whether white, green, oolong or black—is determined by the oxidation levels.

Tea is grown around most of the world in what are called estates, gardens or plantations. Most teas are grown at high altitudes well above pollution levels. Like wines, teas are named for the district in which they are grown. Each district produces teas with distinct qualities and tastes, depending on many factors: including climate, soil, weather conditions, cultivation and processing methods, etc.

Any variety of tea is perfect to incorporate into an individual spiritual practice; as the practice deepens so will the appreciation of this remarkable botanic. Moments spent in quiet reflection, sipping slowly, savouring life, being present in the now—are indeed spiritual. These are ways of creating balance in our lives and this harmony is necessary for finding your bliss.

The wisdoms of the East can easily find a place with the ways of the West. Just as tea spawned a revolution in 1773 in several harbours along the Atlantic Coast, not just the infamous Boston harbour, it can once again launch a revolution—this time a spiritual revolution. This is a new kind of uprising, a true form of rising up, a "wising up," if you will, to what really matters in life and where our true bliss can be found. We're learning that the spiritual accumulation of good in our lives is more important than material acquisitions. The mere recognition of this change in consciousness (awareness) catapults us in a new direction and will lead us straight to the inner realms where our bliss awaits its discovery.

In the East, tea ceremonies represent a balancing of the yin and yang forces. In North America, there is a growing understanding that having the feminine and masculine energies in equality will bring us inner peace. Only when individual inner peace is achieved will world peace ever be possible. Tea has a gentle energy about it, definitely feminine. Coffee, on the other hand, has a more forceful energy, quite masculine. Coffee has its place, as does the male energy. It has never been about which one is better; it is about bringing the two energies (which were once one) back into balance. An imbalance between the feminine and masculine energies has been felt for a very long time now, and in many ways. Our politics, our religions, our businesses, and life in general, have had a dominant masculine energy—almost excluding the feminine entirely.

To create balance, we bring in elements of the energy force that are missing. Tea fits that bill perfectly. No, it doesn't solve all our issues, but it is a step in a positive direction. As much as we pump ourselves up with caffeine and other substances, we must also become creative in the art of slowing ourselves down. In taking the time for reflection and contemplation, we are not as likely to react with judgement or resentment as perhaps we could with an over-stimulated system.

It is all about congruity, the yin and the yang, the masculine and the feminine, in harmony. A spiritual revolution is felt with the heart and is led by Spirit, and no one gets hurt. It is a re-formation, a re-shaping and a re-directing of our lives; and this is all done by choice and done with love. It is a conscious choosing that allows the wisdom of the universe to intercede in our lives; love is a presence that always allows, in all ways. This free-flowing presence of love is like water; it seeps into the tiniest of places if given but the slightest opening. The Source of this love and wisdom dwells within each and every one of us. Tapping into this Source is how we begin loving ourselves and we can do this as easily as steeping ourselves a cup of tea and sipping it in complete surrender and serenity. Ah, the taste of bliss is indeed sweet and accessible to everyone.

"Tea induces a lightness of spirit, clarity of
mind and freedom from all senses of constriction,
whether mental or physical; and promotes such
serenity that mundane cares fall away so that whatever
is strident or exacerbating in daily life can be put
out of your mind for a while."

~ Tea Emperor—Sung Hui Zong ~

Communi-Tea

The earth is my home. All who walk it are my family.
We all come from the same place,
and will return to this holy space.
So here I make my place, in grace, with every race.
We are all one—one with God, one with each other.
In divine community,
we find a commonality and share spirituality.
And we know that God is all there is.
Trivial differences and unimportant
insignificances are released.
As a community, good is all we see,
because good is all we look for—for the good of all.
The good of all begins with the good of me.
I speak clearly, think wholly and live completely in community.
I give thanks to God for the fellowship and
friendship we know as one.
Right here, right now, it starts with me;
companionship, camaraderie with no complexity.
I surrender needing to be right or even to be heard.
I first consider the good of the collaborative
and seek cooperation and correlation.
I let go and let God, and I let live.
We live as one and love as one with the One.
Amen.

"On herbs, there is nothing to resist;
with nothing to resist them. Harmony and balance
do not hide. Entering harmony and balance,
I wash my teacup."

~ The Minister of Leaves ~

Feminini-Tea

In reverence of the feminine force of energy,
I celebrate the femininity of me.
A universe in balance, with stability,
is the home of fertility;
where souls, dreams and spirits grow.
God/Goddess is all there is and all we know.
From this intimacy, tenderness and delicacy
comes a strength of knowing,
a strength of being and a strength of purpose.
The Divine Feminine fortifies my goodness,
my God-ness and the goddess of me.
All that I am embodies and encompasses true femininity,
pure spirituality and total equality.
For all that defines me as female or feminine,
I embody, embrace and express.
The feminine force is gentle and ever flowing;
it is kind and nurturing and ever showing.
I acknowledge the power of creation and give thanks;
gracefully, humbly and blissfully for my femininity.
I release the concerns and fears of feminine verses masculine
and know God as the Ultimate Balance.
I let God give, guide and guard from now on.
Amen.

"Drink your tea slowly and reverently,
as if it is the axis on which the world earth revolves;
slowly, evenly, without rushing toward the future."

~ Thich Nat Hahn ~

Masculini-Tea

With the force and strength of who I am,
I claim all that I am is in perfect balance.
All is in harmony because all is God.
God is all there is. The truth of me has
always been in agreement with this Force.
All facets of me are God, of course;
God expressing through me—God fulfilling me.
This Presence, this Power is one with me;
everything is as it should be.
All that distinguishes me as male or masculine
is divine masculinity in divine harmony.
But this is only one aspect of me.
It is not all that I am,
because all that I am is far grander, far greater.
This makes me good and I see all is good.
Masculinity reaches beyond gender;
right to the heart where all are tender.
For the vastness of me, the divinity of me,
I give thanks to the Creator of all I see.
I let go of all concerns of masculine verses feminine
and find peace in the skin I'm in
and let love guide me all the way.
With pride I let it be—come what may.
Amen.

Affirmation

Nothing outside of me blocks the Force
within me. Self-love sets it free.

Chapter Two

Chi: The Life Force

Affirmation

I clear the way, I open wide.
My gifts I no longer hide.

Chi: The Life Force

"Cha," as we now know, is Japanese for tea. Actually, cha means tea in several different languages. In Japan, sencha is green tea. Directly translated, sen is roasted and cha is tea, making sencha, roasted green tea.

Another similar and familiar word in Chinese is chi (pronounced chee), which means "the life force." Everything that is alive has a life force—humans, animals and plants. This vital force is a non-physical energy that surrounds and circulates through all life forms. In Chinese philosophy, it is believed that this life force is what created the universe. To take away this life force means certain death, while a lagging or blocked life force gives rise to illness and disease.

In Feng Shui (fung shway)—the Chinese art of placement—the life force—chi—is the key component to harmony and balance in the home, the office/work place, and in life. This force must be constantly moving in our lives, but not too quickly or we have chaos, and not too slowly or we become sluggish. Our homes and work places must be free of clutter and obstacles that block this flow of energy. Large pieces of furniture improperly placed will trap and/or block this energy. Stacks of papers, boxes filled with stuff and shoved aside, objects hidden or misplaced, broken things, unfinished projects, unsafe areas, etc.—all these things weigh heavily on us. They become overwhelming things "to-do" and end up blocking this life force and thus prevent the free flow of energy.

Chi can easily be seen as the God Force in our lives. Are we allowing this Force into our daily activities or are we hindering it? By handling the clutter and disorder of our lives, we invite the God Force to flow naturally and easily into all our affairs. But this is more than the physical backlog of the things that surround us; it is a spiritual and emotional unclogging that allows this Force to flow freely. Locked up (and blocked up) within us, usually in our minds but also in our hearts, are a lot of false beliefs, limiting ideas, negative thoughts and often, some very haunting memories, all of which contribute to low self-esteem and very little self-love. These are old programs—things we haven't released, things we haven't forgiven—that we keep replaying over and over. We have the power to eliminate these programs—things we haven't released, things we haven't forgiven—that we keep replaying over and over. We have the power to eliminate these programs. No one holds the controls but us—and this is how we claim our bliss.

These thoughts of fear and uncertainty are the ramblings of what can be referred to as the "lower mind." Once we are able to eliminate them or come to peace with them, we will find ourselves in touch with the Higher Mind, which is another term for the God Force, the Life Force. This Force is neither masculine nor feminine, although traditionally we have heard God referred to in the masculine. It really matters not; whatever one finds comfort with is what we are seeking here. A mind at peace, a heart open to love, a body in good health, and a soul with a clear path to God—now this is BLISS, and we can all have it.

This is why we create a Spiritual Practice for our lives; or we could just call it, moments for loving ourselves. Some feel that a spiritual practice involves a great deal of discipline, and this is a word that brings up a lot of resistance in many people. The very thought of discipline evokes images and feelings of pain and punishment. We are not going there though; that is not our focus——love is our focus.

A spiritual practice simply means gradually incorporating spiritual behaviours, actions and/or methods into our daily lives. Such activities might include praying, meditating, reciting positive affirmations, reading inspirational writings and poetry, or just spending time in quiet contemplation. Part of a spiritual practice might include listening to or making music, walking in nature, or simply breathing deeply. It might involve singing or chanting or dancing or yoga—anything that brings peace of mind and tender moments of love and gratitude. It can be as easy as sitting down with a cup of tea and being totally present in the moment—cha for chi, tea for energy.

A loving, spiritual practice begins by setting aside certain times of the day that fit into one's life easily, keeping it simple and comfortable to start with. Each one of us is unique, and we will find enjoyment in different ways. This is a practice we tailor-make for our own individual lifestyle, knowing that our practice can be changed when things change—which they inevitably do. The point is—just start doing something! Start loving YOURSELF.

It is called spiritual practice, not spiritual perfection. If a day is missed, we do not beat ourselves up emotionally; we simply start again. God is always there, always available, any time of the day or night. Whatever moment we choose is perfect—just as we are, in God's eyes. It is our own perfection we will learn to see by incorporating and opening up to these loving spiritual activities in our everyday lives.

Our spiritual practice is how we fill ourselves up with love when life starts to drain us. By making it part of our daily routine, our resources will remain plentiful. No one and no *thing* can take away our life force, our God Force, because it is the very essence of whom we are. Love is the essence of who we are. God and love are interchangeable, just as self-love and BLISS are. As we fill the cup with tea we can see it as ourselves being refilled.

When entering into any spiritual activity, it is important to remember to enter in wholeness. This is not about a broken or less-than self—there is already enough out there that says we need to be fixed. This is about accepting and embracing all that we truly are. It is about releasing old beliefs, reclaiming our power, recharging ourselves, and loving ourselves. It is about living in joy, not reliving our so-called mistakes. It is about remembering God and surrendering to the God Force, because this is where and when we find inner peace and true BLISS.

In our spiritual practice, we come not from the ego—the lower mind—but from our God Self, our Higher Self—the Higher Mind. The capital "S" of Self merges in harmony with the small "s" of the human self—God and human in perfect order, divine harmony, one with the One. Now this adds a new and deeper meaning to BLISS.

No, our spiritual practice is not about a tough discipline; it is more about determination, dedication and devotion. These words sound much nicer, and they suggest a more pleasant undertaking but still indicate a discipline of sorts in that we are retraining ourselves. And if we slack off or forget, there is no need for guilt or lamenting. We simply start again. We remember our determination, and we remind ourselves that we do indeed deserve it, and we begin the training and self-loving process again.

God keeps no scorecard and neither should we. Soon our spiritual practice will become so stimulating and relaxing—yes, both at the same time—that we will not want to miss it for any reason. It doesn't require a strict time and place and can start simply. A few moments of prayer in a traffic jam, several deep breaths before entering the boardroom, a few affirmations in front of the mirror in the morning—these simple spiritual actions can completely transform the energy, relieve stress, and uplift the day. Quiet moments holding a sleeping baby, stroking a cat curled up on one's lap, sharing the elation with a child over a hard-earned achievement at school—all these precious moments of gratitude elevate us to a place of peace and contentment. We can incorporate so much of everyday life into our spiritual practice as long as we stay awake and aware, and remember that it is all about love.

Our power lies only in the now. No power comes from dwelling on the past or worrying about the future. So we can start simply by just being present in the moment; that makes the transition into dedicated moments of stillness much easier. It is amazing how quickly an hour of quiet time can go by. Whatever works, the goal is to just start doing it. God is incredibly patient, and part of our learning is to be patient and loving with ourselves. Fifteen mindful moments with a cup of tea can and will change your life.

As much as possible, be not afraid nor in a hurry, for that defeats the purpose. The Force is within us, and it is vital to every one of us. Moments of tranquility allow this Force, this Power, to be felt; these are indeed moments of empowerment. Who among us is not looking for that? Needing that Self-awareness, longing for a glimpse into enlightenment, whatever that means, and yearning for Self-love, which is also self-love, God's love in combination with our own love of self. We won't know until we make ourselves available to it.

The Force is with us, all of us, because It is us. We are all together on this sacred journey of Self-love—all for One and one for All.

"One should clean out a room in
one's home and place only a tea table and a chair
in the room with some boiled water and fragrant tea.
Afterwards, sit solitarily
and allow one's spirit to become tranquil,
light and natural."

~ Li Ri Hua— A Ming Dynasty Scholar ~

Dei-Tea

Omnipotent, Omnipresent, Omniscient;
All-Powerful, Ever-Present, Infinitely Knowledgeable.
God knows all, sees all, and is All.
I celebrate in the knowing that God
is all there is and ever will be.
I quietly and confidently take myself
to the place where we are one.
From this divine place within,
I can accept myself for who I truly am.
I am good and pure, whole and secure.
In my power, with all my wisdom,
I am grateful to this Eternal Force.
A Power that knows many names
but is only One——a pure and infinite One.
No limits—no boundaries—no place where God is not.
To the Light of the World, the Holy and Hallowed,
the Almighty and the Altruistic, the Sacred and the Sacrosanct;
I trust it all over to you and I am sanctified.
I live and let live by your grace and I am purified.
A deity whose love cannot be denied.
I accept this, I trust this, and so it is.
Amen.

"Tea . . . is a religion of the art of life."

~ Okakura ~

Receptivi-Tea

I am a receptacle for God.
God is the life force I hold within me.
This power is all there is, and we are one.
I make myself ready, I clear the way, and it is done.
I am now able to receive
God in unlimited amounts—I treasure all that I have.
But it is the giving and receiving that counts.
What God gives me I share with others because I know
there is always more.
I celebrate all my gifts and all that is good.
The enormity of this Force is now understood.
There is ebb and flow, and I am constantly refilled.
I am appreciative and receptive; I am open and caring.
This is how I choose to live.
I thank the Divine Giver for the gifts we are sharing.
I sense with a new way of knowing.
I am allowing and willing and my open heart is showing.
The giver and the receiver are one and the same.
I reach out. I reach in.
I receive and I am relieved.
I say it is so, and I say it in your name.
It is done, and joy I claim.
Amen.

"The flavor of Zen and the
flavor of tea is the same."

~Japanese Proverb ~

Uni-Tea

Me multiplied by God equals God.
God is all there is.
We are one; one is all we can be.
This is divine unity.
God is the Whole; I am a part of the Whole.
Our union is divine; our integration is for all time.
Forever unified—unity for eternity.
We are in agreement; our elements are in harmony.
We live and move and have our being as one,
inseparable and indivisible.
No thought, no word, no action—can prevent our unity.
This is how we form a community and raise consciousness.
Nothing, NO THING, can take us from our goodness.
God's strength is our power; it is what unites us all.
In integration there is no separation and no segregation.
We do not lack for any *thing*,
and we thank God for every *thing*.
We trust this Force and release all else.
It is done as we claim it to be and we do so in unity.
Amen.

Affirmation

I now choose to set free
all that I was created to be.

Chapter Three

Choosing To Choose

Affirmation

With the freedom of choice,
I find a new voice.
And I use it.

Choosing To Choose

We are meant to experience joy on this glorious and sacred journey we are all on. Joy is part of our divine nature; it is one of the gifts God has graced us with. However, we have to be willing to accept this gift.

There is a difference between joy and happiness. Both are essential to life, and neither has anything to do with luck. Nor can we rely on someone else to provide us with either one. Others can certainly enhance the quality of our lives, just as we can enrich the lives of others. Ah, but to know both joy and happiness is to know the bliss of self-love which brings true inner peace.

Joy is connected with the soul, in that it is felt from deep down inside. Happiness can be a tad on the superficial side, in that we may look to people or things or events to bring us temporary happiness. Some will spend a lifetime addicted to the high of temporary happiness and will always be chasing something or someone. We deserve much more than momentary gratification. We are each worthy of the contentment that self-love, true success, brings. This enduring sense of serenity is indeed blissful, and this bliss can be felt when we connect with the love of the Divine Force within.

Yes, the trials and tribulations of everyday life can drain one of joy, bliss, self-love, and all the other good stuff, but only if we let it. Sometimes all we need is a few fleeting seconds of this bliss to remind us that we are not alone and that we all deserve to love and be loved. This is different from the happiness that vanishes after an event or an encounter; this little flash of remembrance is deep and profound and felt by the heart.

Bliss, this place of inner tranquility and self-love usually comes through surrendering—when we stop fighting our divine nature. It is our natural make up, our original condition—to be loving— we just weren't taught to start with ourselves. Or were we?

"Love thyself." "Love thy neighbour as thyself." Oh, that does sound familiar, doesn't it?

Perhaps this is why we have had, and, are currently facing issues about loving our neighbour and we choose to go to war with the ones we could be loving. We need to love ourselves first, and, foremost. Loving ourselves can be as simple as going out in nature for walk and can come from something as simple as cupping a flower and inhaling deeply. Loving ourselves can be done in the time it takes to mindfully sip a freshly-steeped cup of tea. We do have choices.

If either joy or happiness has been elusive in our lives, we are wise to ask ourselves, "Why?" First of all, we simply have to believe that God wants each and every one of us to be happy and to know the joy of self-love and bliss. We have not come here to suffer. Suffering may be how some of us choose to learn life's lessons, but it need not be a permanent condition. We can choose to learn without suffering—by allowing ourselves to believe it is possible. Then, we can learn to love ourselves both in the good times and through our times of agony, knowing that the tough times are showing us something about who we are and how vital it is to remain in a place of love.

One of the greatest revelations we can have is knowing that we all have choices; oodles and oodles of choices. We may think back to a time when it seemed we had no choice. Yet when we explore more deeply, and time blesses us with clarity of mind, and we decide whether we were coming from a place of love or not, we can usually see how many other choices we actually could have had. We do not have to spend time looking back to pinpoint every situation we wish would have gone differently. The truth is: we only have now and now is when we choose to choose—and choose to start mindfully loving ourselves and finding our bliss.

We can make the decision this very moment—to be open to love—and to all the choices we really do have. If at times it seems we have only one choice, this is a good indication that we have shut ourselves off from our divine nature. In these moments, it is essential to reconnect—to take the time to breathe, to get quiet and to ask for help. God is always available. In surrendering the situation, we give it up, and in no time we will begin to see other choices. There will be no more, *I have no money; there is nothing else I can do.* This turns into, *I have no money, God; what else can I do?* As we open and allow something will reveal itself.

If we have chosen jobs or relationships that no longer serve us, then we serve ourselves best by choosing to choose something else. In releasing the belief that we have no other choices, we take a giant leap of faith into a life of happiness, joy, and BLISS. Alternatively, we can choose to see our jobs or our relationships in another way. If we can be bold enough to ask ourselves if we are really putting all of what we have into them—the jobs or the relationships—might we not be having a very different experience of them? Are we truly loving ourselves in both or either of these experiences if we are not putting all we have into them?

Every decision we have ever made in life was truly based on one thing—how much we loved ourselves at the time of making that choice.

We trap ourselves in little boxes with labels that say, *not enough education,* or *not good-looking enough,* or ones that just say, *not good enough,* [period], and this is how we end up limiting our choices, and thus, our lives. The limited amount of self-love we have had for ourselves reads like a road map on the journey to nowhere. Sometimes we allow others to put us in boxes, like the one that says, *won't ever amount to much,* or that ever-so-tiny box that says, *doesn't deserve it.* What is this box, really? And what is the label? It says, *I don't love me, I am trapped, I have no purpose, and I am dying a little every day.* In this very limited space of no love of self, we begin to choke and gasp for something more. No one deserves this; it is time to set ourselves free.

With the freedom of self-love we are given the simple miracle of using our higher minds to make conscious choices out of awareness and are no longer tuned out or shut down. Making the choices with the best outcomes is never guaranteed, but using the freedom of choice along with self-love to make all decisions sheds a new light on the situation—God's light. We often say that God has given us free will, but then we choose not to use it!

There are no walls on the boxes that hold us back; it is we who have chosen to see the barriers as real. With the eyes of love closed, the barriers even feel real. Not everyone is born rich or gorgeous or with genius status, but we are all born with free will and we are all born with the ability to love endlessly. We have all heard numerous rags-to-riches stories and happily-ever-after stories; but this is the story of our lives and it is indeed a love story. What kind of lead character are we going to choose to play?

This is not just about a happy ending; it is about a happy journey, a happy life—a life filled with love and bliss. We start by creating this happy story in our minds, and if stuff happens, we get to take the character in another direction. We can choose the path of light and love or the dark route of doubt and deceit. The choice is ours; it always has been and it always will be.

We can also choose not to choose, but this is your life, so why not choose to be happy? Why not choose to know happiness and choose to know the joy of love? For in these, there is God, this is where we find bliss and true success.

Affirmation

I choose to choose.
From now on I choose me.

"Teaism is a cult
founded on the adoration of the beautiful
among the sordid facts of everyday existence.
It inculcates purity and harmony,
the mystery of mutual charity,
the romanticism of the social order."

~ Okakura Kakuzo ~

Sereni-Tea

In peaceful repose, I breathe in all that I am.
I marvel at the simplicity and purity of divine serenity.
From this place of perfection I am undisturbed.
I am calm and refreshed, most unperturbed.
I see God, I feel God, I hear the word.
Clearly and calmly, I am one with this Force.
I am intact; I am whole, pure and good.
I see the reflection of my own perfection; no defects
and no deficiencies.
Nothing can diminish the goodness
and the God-ness of me.
In serenity and with deep gratitude,
and along with each sip of tea
I realize God is all of me from within me.
And this is my place of bliss—
from here I can do and be anything.
So with ease and grace I surrender my pace.
I have nothing to fear; there is no race.
No rush, no hurry, no finish line.
Every day I know victory in the arms of the Divine;
my giver, my deliverer, the provider of bliss.
I need for nothing; the aches are all gone.
My soul is free to be all that it is—love is all it can be,
and that's good enough for me.
Amen.

"If you are cold, tea will warm you;
if you are too heated, it will cool you;
if you are depressed, it will cheer you;
if you are exhausted, it will calm you."

~ William Gladstone ~

Felici-Tea

My comfort and contentment
come from a place of bliss.
The bright buoyancy I've been blessed with
belongs to the Divine.
Bestowed on me at birth,
this felicitous agreement is Heaven-sent.
All the joy I know comes right from God.
God is all there is. One with God, I am content.
I open and rejoice.   I receive and I am relieved.
All worry gone and fear released,
I make room for the presence of the Divine Presence.
The Force is joy; the Source is joy.
Joy in its grandest sense, its most genuine sense,
in its original sense.
Pure and good, unharmed and unimpaired,
my heart is now ready.
With reverence and humility
I accept this divine felicity.
By the grace of God and the glory of God,
I let go to God and guardianship.
I go in God and glow with God and I radiate
happiness and bliss; and no joy do I miss.
I claim it all. I claim it to be.
And so it is for me.
Amen.

"For tea, though ridiculed by those who are naturally nervous in their sensibilities, or are become so from wine-drinking, and are not susceptible of influence from so refined a stimulant, will always be the favored beverage of the intellectual."

~ Thomas Quincy ~

Festivi-Tea

There is so much to celebrate.
Every moment in God is an eternity of joy.
Every moment with God is an infinity of delight.
I let go of time and rejoice in the now.
In the power of this moment, God shows me how.
I am one with the Source of this jubilation,
the provider of this soul celebration.
One with divine revelry is all we really can be.
I exult in my own goodness and my own worthiness.
I have been given an invitation to celebrate all the time.
I claim back the gifts that once were mine.
With jubilee, I thank God for the wonders
and joys of our divine unity.
Every day is a special occasion and a reason for celebration.
Every breath is a pleasure, an ecstasy,
an inspiration of divinity.
I have nothing to plan or prepare,
I surrender to the Divine Host, who is always there.
The party is for me, and these gifts I share—my light,
my love, my laughter.
I know the truth of happily ever after.
Amen.

Affirmation

I pray from a new place
and feel the presence of grace.

Chapter Four

Choosing Prayer for the Mind

Affirmation

With my mind I journey to
a place of peace.
I know this place,
I have been here before.

Choosing Prayer for the Mind

The unlimited power of the mind comes directly from an endless source: God. What ends up limiting our lives and our minds are the thoughts that are kept alive and fed by the *lower mind*. Our thoughts end up ruling our lives; they can and do take on a life of their own, as well as a vibration of their own. Many of these are nagging and negative thoughts, unloving thoughts. Keeping them afloat takes the wind out of our sails, and we end up being robbed of our own joy and drifting aimlessly. Some of us have become very good at hiding the self-doubt that these thoughts produce. This self-doubt is really a lack of self-love and a true misunderstanding of who we really are. Then we wonder why things don't turn out as we hoped they would.

If our lives aren't all that we want them to be right now, this might be the opportunity to make some changes. This moment, in this very second, we have the choice to decide how we want our lives to be.

This is not about winning the lottery—this is about taking charge of the thoughts that are going on in our heads. Nor is it about being in control. We are using that phrase incorrectly most of the time, thinking that if we control every moment of every day, then we have accomplished something great.

But *being in control* does not allow any room for God. If we have everything under control, how can God assist us?

This is about surrender—pure and sweet surrender. And with a good, hot cup of tea, we can begin the surrendering process, one sip, one breath, and one thought at a time. This is one way we can let go of the thoughts we have been dragging around—our own negative and denying thoughts that have been keeping us down; unloving thoughts about our very own selves.

Only when our thoughts change will our lives change.

One of the first thoughts to go is that we don't deserve good in our lives. We have to get our thinking straight on that one right now. We are, first and foremost, children of God; this is where our good comes from. And from good comes joy, happiness, inner peace and self-love, and this is the gift of bliss. We are offered these gifts right from birth and no one can ever take them away. Some of us didn't even know these gifts were for us. We thought they must have someone else's names on them because we hadn't done anything to deserve them. This is one of the great paradoxes of this life. We don't have to do anything to earn or deserve love—love of self, love from another and love for another.

Oh, how hard it seems to swallow that! We have been taught some challenging lessons about who wins in this world. Most of us believe it is someone else—that they must be saints or that they must be crooks, but they are never *simple little ol' me.* How can we all win? Let's start by getting clear on what it is we want to win, what the real prize is.

Sadly, in our North American culture, many of us are chasing after things we believe will bring us happiness but do not. We have gotten a little sidetracked on what deems us to be successful. Number one seems to be money. Power, prestige and popularity are right up there also, but what are they?

What if it was much simpler and the real prizes were love, inner peace, joy, self-worth, integrity, passion and purpose? The true 'jackpot' is discovering your bliss.

All that may sound namby-pamby, but if we had all those things, the mind would be a sanctuary, a pristine walk in a rose garden, fragrant and fulfilling.

So how come most of us feel we are getting stabbed by the thorns instead? The roses are there, but they are withered and scraggly, because no one has been taking care of them. They are overrun with weeds and bugs.

Negativity, doubt and lack of self-love are the weeds that are choking the beautiful flowers of God. The bugs of confusion and frustration are eating away at the exquisite blossoms of God's rose bushes. There is no gardener to hire to clean it all up. It is up to each of us to begin pulling out the weeds, one at a time, getting rid of all those negative thoughts, the ones that are choking the life out of the children of God. Love is all the children of God seek because love is all they know. We must become the keepers of our own gardens, our own minds, and not worry about anybody else's. We tend to our own first. We begin all of this by relearning how to love and accept ourselves— simply because we are children of God.

Where do we begin? Choosing prayer for the mind is an excellent way to create inner peace and to be at peace with all that is happening in our heads. Bliss comes from inner peace.

Many of us have been taught to pray in one fashion or another. Prayer is very personal and needs to be respected. If more of us prayed on a regular basis, we would surely be gentler with ourselves, and then ultimately kinder to each other.

Most of us seem to be more comfortable praying in silence in our heads, with our thoughts, rather than out loud. That is because there is something deep within us that knows our words are being heard or felt by some power source somewhere.

What if that source dwelled within each and every one of us? We have often heard the statement, "The Kingdom of Heaven is within." And we just know that God lives in Heaven. So if God lives within us, then all our thoughts are heard all the time—the positive and the negative alike. That is why choosing prayer for the mind is so important. What a powerful thought that is: *God lives in me. God loves me.* This is where our strength comes from. If we have been limiting ourselves with our old beliefs and lack of self-love, then we have been limiting God and not loving God.

Prayer is about mentally and spiritually taking our power back, and doing so from a place of love. It is about claiming it, owning it, and being responsible for it and with it. It is not about pleading, begging or bargaining. None of this *Please, please God*, or *if you'll do this one thing for me I'll go to church forever.* All of this is praying from a place of powerlessness, desperation, and from a place of very little love. If we believe we are less, we will experience life in that manner. This is not at all about settling for less. This is about claiming all the love we deserve to have—for ourselves first and then sharing this love with everyone we meet.

When opening up to the power of prayer, it's important to be open to praying itself. If we feel that what we have been doing in the past hasn't been working, then perhaps it's time to try a different way. It doesn't make "wrong" anything we have done in the past; it simply means adjusting our approach and the energy behind our prayers. Beginning from a place of love and celebration definitely changes the energy. When praying from a place of power and gratitude, we are not separate from God. When we choose to make praying a part of our daily lives, we move to the place of oneness. This oneness has always existed; it is just that we disconnected ourselves from it by all the distractions in our lives and all the deterring thoughts in our minds.

How do we reconnect? We simply reach out, (or in) to God through our prayers—by talking to God and expressing freely. Start by communicating, just as one does with a person they love and need to talk to. Be precise. Ask specifically for what is desired. And most importantly, believe. Believe in God and the power of the God Force within, and celebrate that power, for it is who we really are; and in that, we are reconnected in love. When we pray, we pray that what we desire is already here, that we have it, whatever "it" may be—that it is already done. And we start with *Thank you. Thank you for the steady flow of income in my life now. Thank you for this miraculous healing. I am so grateful for this special person who has come into my life.*

Praying may be new to some, but just as in school, we learn by practice and repetition. Have fun with it and see how exciting praying can become. Having all our dreams come true in our minds first is indeed a loving celebration of self. If we can't see it, it won't happen. Starting with *Thank you* instead of pleading with *please, please,* immediately puts us in a position of love and strength rather than ineptitude.

We came here to enjoy this life. So if joy has eluded us, waste no time on who did what or said what. Let go of blame and start choosing new thoughts. Start simply with *I am good, I am loveable, I deserve to be happy,* and *life is great.* Then keep expanding these thoughts and setting aside time each day for a few moments of reconnecting from a place of love. These moments in oneness with God are indeed moments of celebration. Jesus said, "It is done unto us as we believe," so believe in good, believe in the power of positive thought, believe in God, and—here's the big one—love and believe in yourself!

Our prayers matter. Our thoughts matter. They matter greatly and significantly. Every thought has a consequence. It's not just the act or the word but the very thought itself that has an outcome, that has an effect. Loving thoughts are even more powerful.

We are so blessed that we get to choose, that we get to reconnect with God through our thoughts and our prayers. So let's pray every chance we get—not just in church but at work, in the car, in bed, on the beach, in line at the bank, waiting for the bus, while walking the dog. God is within us, God is wherever we are.

Imagine a world where happy, loving thoughts rise above all other thought patterns—where negativity diminishes, and thereafter, feel and witness a world in greater harmony.

See each exquisite blossom in God's garden opening to share its precious beauty and uniqueness with the entire world. Now this is a reason to celebrate and a way to begin the journey back to love. It all starts with one. Be the one—be one who loves yourself and has found your bliss.

"Tea tempers the spirits and harmonizes the mind,
dispels lassitude and relieves fatigue,
awakens thought and prevents drowsiness,
lightens or refreshes the body,
and clears the perceptive faculties."

~ Lu Yu – Chinese Poet ~

Accountabili-Tea

For my actions I claim responsibility.
I hold myself lovingly in that accountability.
Every thought, word and deed has a consequence.
It is all now, there is no past tense.
God is the now, God is all there is.
We are one right now. Yesterday is gone.
Today I accept the good and become the good.
I blame no one and give no one charge over me.
I live in divine accountability.
All I reap, I shall sow. All I think is all I know.
I know good, I do good, I am good.
In my power I proudly stand.
I walk tall with God, hand in hand;
heart to heart, soul to Spirit, One with all.
I am not alone. One for All and all for the One.
Knowing this, I live gratefully and g
racefully and I thank God faithfully.
It rarely becomes too much for me.
In the now God shows me how.
I surrender, I give in.
I let go and let God begin;
again and again.
Amen.

"Each and every cup represents an imaginary voyage."

~ Catherine Douzel ~

Reciproci-Tea

God gives and returns to me from within me.
I look out, I look in, and God is all I see.
God is all there is.
Eternal giving and eternal receiving;
together they work in complete harmony.
Like a dance choreographed so beautifully.
We flow together, live together,
move and have our being as one.
This interchange is mutual and divine and mine.
I claim it. I claim God for me and all that is good for me.
All I sow, I shall reap—this is God's law.
Love and goodness manifest for me now.
To take back or take away is never God's way.
I choose my words and thoughts carefully.
I pray from a place of security and unity.
I respect God's laws of reciprocity and generosity.
I am grateful for this rule, for the way it is.
I remember to surrender and trust what is,
I have faith in how things will come back to me.
And so they do, and so it is,
and so I let it be and that is reciprocity.
Amen.

"My dear, if you could give me a cup of tea to clear my muddle of a head, I should better understand your affairs."

~ Charles Dickens ~

Sani-Tea

Once again, I wake up and come to my senses.
I let go and move into my divine right mind.
It is one with the One Mind; the Infinite Mind,
the mind of us all.
I keep things simple, and peace I find.
God is all there is. We are one of a kind.
The universe now responds to my mental state.
I am calm, collected and reconnected.
What I think I now set into being.
I am good, life is good, and God is good.
With the One Mind I have peace of mind.
I have a good mind and a solid mind.
Mind over matter, if I don't mind, it doesn't matter.
What I put my mind to is what appears in my life.
I give thanks and trust this Infinite Intelligence
that guides and guards me and now makes sense.
I rest my mind; I arrest my thoughts
and give my best to all that is sought.
Everything else is not up to me.
I give it to God, and I let it be. And it is all good.
What else could it be?
Amen.

Affirmation

My soul is warm and soothing,
I am caressed and cared for.

Chapter Five

Choosing Meditation for the Soul

Affirmation

My soul knows me—we have a history.
I know my soul; it is now free to be.

Choosing Meditation for the Soul

It has been said that prayer is *talking* to God and meditation is *listening* to God. Going from prayer into meditation can be very empowering. God listens to us; we listen to God. This sounds like a good relationship. One of the purposes of meditating is simply to clear away the mind clutter to make room for God. Making room for God is making room for love—this is how to begin loving the self—it is a nurturing of the self.

For some of us, meditation conjures up all kinds of images of discomfort and distortion. That is not what we're trying to accomplish here. We can keep this simple, calling it quiet time—time for self-love. Meditation is a calming of the mind. It is setting aside time to become aware of all that is going on in our heads and to consciously release it all to create peace—peace of mind. We begin by recognizing all the voices that still want to be heard. They may be the voices of our parents, our teachers, our siblings, our religious leaders, the newscasters, our friends, etc. We need to quiet the voices of these other people; for there is only one voice we are longing to hear: the voice of God—the melody of love.

There is another strong voice we hear—our own. This voice often speaks to us critically, pointing out our inadequacies and presumed mistakes—and what voice is this? This is the sound of a voice that has not yet found love. Meditation can move us from that lower level of the mind into the higher level where the voice of God can be heard and felt. Sometimes it is only felt, but this in itself is a wonderful experience—this is what it feels like to be loved—by yourself; your higher self.

It's important to take time to still all the unloving voices. Those outside voices need no longer haunt us nor hinder us.

As adults we can now realize that a lot is said in anger, out of fear and ignorance, and from confusion and frustration—all of these are unloving places. Just as we may have said negative and unloving things to others that we wished we had not, perhaps they may be wishing the same thing, too. We need to release all the voices that are still lingering. Hanging on to any of them only serves to limit love—our capability to love and to be loved fully; as well as the ability to truly love ourselves.

Meditation has many purposes but let us begin by seeing it as a means for opening ourselves up to the power of God, and since God is love, we open to the power of love. Of course, this is our choice. God forces no one but is always ready when we make the decision to open up and to love ourselves; for this is what our whole journey is about.

In meditation we begin to expand and those moments given to God are indeed the greatest gift we can ever give back. It's all about giving and receiving, for in truth, they are one and the same.

There are a lot of things going on beyond the conscious mind. The conscious mind is what we now have chosen to be at peace with, to pray with, to provide the power to draw only good into our lives and to begin the wonderful process of learning to love ourselves and find our bliss. There is something intrinsic within us, about us, that connects us all—something we tap into frequently or infrequently, consciously or subconsciously. Could that be the mysterious soul we all hear about? Perhaps, if we believe it is, then that is all that matters.

The soul is a force within us; it is our God connection. Some feel the soul is connected with the mind; some believe it has a connection to the heart. Let's just trust that God will know exactly what to do when we make ourselves available for love. A path made clear from the heart, to the mind, to God, seems like the ultimate route to take. Let's also remember to make it a two-way path.

Is this not the mind-body-soul connection everyone talks about? Or is it mind-body-spirit? Soul is God; Spirit is God. God is all there is and allows us to know ourselves and to love ourselves—if we choose, if we remember, and if we ask. "Ask and you will receive."

Maybe what is out there, or within us, is just too big to comprehend. Yes, it certainly could be, but we do not sell ourselves short by saying, *I'll never get it*. The fact is, we've already got "It"—whatever and however big "It" is. Maybe we'll get all we need and nothing more, but also nothing less than we need either. We are the ones who ultimately choose how much, by continuing to ask and by maintaining trust and living in love, by moving ahead with what feels right and what feels like God. Isn't that what we are all seeking—a feeling, a knowing, a satisfaction? And are all these things not God? So we are all seeking God, and God is right here; there is no place that God is not. The In-Dweller, All-Knowing, Absolute, the I AM, the Presence, the Power—whatever term we choose, or however many fit.

This is about choosing to have a strong relationship with God—by creating and nurturing and deepening that connection. It's about being active, pro-active; and it's about being still, listening, observing—paying mind. Making time, taking time and stopping time. All of these are indeed how we love ourselves; a little at a time.

We take time with a cup of tea, enjoying it one sip at a time, one deep inhalation after another. No rush, no expectations, just simple surrender. This is how we celebrate God—with little gestures of thanks and moments of recognition on a regular basis, and not just when things are going great.

It will take some time to quiet all the voices and thoughts going on in our heads; some have lived there a long time. Do we ever reach moments of no thought—just blissful stillness where we visit some other dimension? Perhaps, but we need not worry if that does not happen. As the thoughts come during our quiet times, we simply recognize them, and lovingly, send them on their way. Some thoughts we need to be firm with whenever they appear. If they are hindrances, we have the power to dismiss them entirely.

Some like to meditate by reciting phrases over and over in the mind or out loud. Simple ones like, *God is love* or *Peace be with us*—whatever feels right. This may be a good way to get started, for these simple statements do cut down on the mind chatter and also become chant-like and can help take the mind into somewhat of a trance state. From this state of being the soul can express its freedom. All of this takes practice but can be very fulfilling at the same time. And yes, it will even take practice to just sit still.

There is no wrong way to meditate. Deep breathe to relax and then move into the quiet space of your mind. Some people are very visual and create lush gardens full of detail with plenty to see as they remain quiet. Others go to the beach, in their minds, and listen to the pounding of the waves. The place we create is peaceful and soothing; that is all it needs to be. From this quiet place, we can acknowledge the soul, God, the angels, the Holy Spirit, and loved ones who have passed away, and say hello to them all. If we let them know we are here, they may have something to say to us, something we would never get to hear with all the activities of our busy lives.

Breathing deeply and concentrating on the sound of the breath also helps diminish the gibberish of a busy lower mind. These are ways to build a relationship with God and with our soul, although they probably are one and the same. All of this is self-love; loving the self. We even get to choose what kind of relationship we want with God. Do we want a God who forgives, accepts, allows, teaches, nurtures, encourages and loves us? Whatever we ask for, we shall have. We just have to believe—to believe in a God that believes in us no matter what, no matter how long it has been. For in the end, we go back to God. How nice it would be to have established a sound relationship ahead of time. But in the now, there is only God, and now is when we choose to enhance this partnership by loving ourselves.

Meditation is not just good for the soul, but also the mind, the body and the heart. Love penetrates every fiber of our being and contributes to our well-being. This is a gift we give to ourselves. The simple gift of time reconnects us to something so great, so powerful and so fulfilling that it warrants at least a valiant attempt. Nothing goes unrewarded, even simple moments of gratitude are a recognition and a celebration of all that is. They are a celebration of Self—the Divine Self within us as well as our human self.

Often when a longing from deep inside us surfaces, we don't know how to satisfy it. We try to fill it with something outside of ourselves: food, drugs, cigarettes, alcohol, sex, gambling, shopping, crime—the list goes on. We do these things in an unconscious attempt to appease the yearning or to sedate the aching, when all that this unnamable desire seeks is to be—to simply BE.

In meditation, we acknowledge this desire, we celebrate it and we welcome it, because it is who we really are. It is the God presence within us. We put no shame and guilt on the behaviours we have chosen in the past to suppress this inclination. This is a new day, and we now choose a new way. We seek more than the temporary and superficial happiness or satisfaction we felt those actions provided. We seek, instead, wholeness and completeness, which we will only find in God, and in the moments—the precious moments—we give to God. This is self-love at its finest.

Meditation helps us to break the cycle of self-destructive, unloving behaviours and thought patterns. It helps us to know that God created us good, all of us, not just a select few. If we cannot see the good in ourselves, how on earth can we expect others to see it, and how will we see it in others? If we cannot love ourselves how can we expect others to love us and to have deep, fulfilling relationships? If good and love are restricted by our thoughts and beliefs, so will the joy in our lives be limited.

None of us have been short-changed. When we come to each other in wholeness, we have a much greater chance for successful and ever-growing relationships. If we believe we have something missing and look to another to keep us intact, we put undue stress on that relationship right from the beginning. If the other person feels they, too, have missing pieces, the burden can be too great to bear. This is why loving the self is so vital and so necessary in our lives and for our lives.

In moments of deliberate stillness, we connect the pieces, not collect them. We have always had them; they were just misaligned. We have all tried to fit puzzle pieces into places we knew they didn't belong. Just as we intuitively know when we are not in the best relationship or job or are on a path of self-destruction. We have to trust that no pieces are missing and that if we just keep going and growing, and loving, we'll see the whole picture.

The world will be a quieter and gentler home when we all start to realize our own power, our own innate spiritual qualities; our God-like gifts. The belief that we are separate from each other and from God has served no one, no thing, and certainly not the human race, nor this planet. It was only out of our perceived inadequacies and lack of self-love that we chose to assert ourselves over one another. Only in our feelings of detachment did we choose ways of hurting each other, all in an attempt to feel better about ourselves. That's quite ironic when we truly think about it. Isn't it?

Now that we know we are all one and one with God and that loving ourselves is the answer—what are we going to do to find our bliss? Ideally, we start by tuning in to the inner wisdom we all possess. We each have our own power source to tap into, although we know all the power comes from the same Source. This Source is limitless. In quiet time, we hook up and into this Source, recharging ourselves and reacquainting ourselves with who we truly are. Thus, we enhance our relationship with God, with soul, with ourselves—which again, are one and the same. We do not need anyone else to assist us in this process. We have the power, God's power, anytime we request it. This is how we claim our power—quietly, calmly, lovingly, in sweet surrender to God.

There is a lot of mystery surrounding the soul and even more unanswered questions. Perhaps the soul has had many experiences here and elsewhere, and if so, there is a lot of wisdom and a great deal of love in each and every one of us. Meditation is one way of accessing this wise inner presence and this connection with God. God will always light our path, no matter how dark it was where we were before. We own our power when we choose to live in the light of love. We celebrate our strength and wisdom by getting quiet and allowing the glory of God to be. Oh, yes, this is self-love and true BLISS.

"Tea does our fancy aid, represses those vapours which the head invade, and keeps that palace of the soul serene."

~ Edmund Waller ~

Infini-Tea

So great are the gifts of God
that they cannot be measured.
Absolute, boundless perfection is the God I know,
and I know that God is all there is.
The Force is infinite.
There is no space between God and me—we are one.
This Oneness is immeasurable and immutable.
Infinite love is given to me free of any conditions,
free of any limits and free of all boundaries.
I am good enough to accept and embody God's love just as I am.
A love for eternity from Divine Infinity,
is the greatest treasure of all.
For this gift, I feel from the core of my being
a love and appreciation beyond words.
God knows the home of love and gratitude,
this place that defies borders and
this place where words do not exist.
This is the birthplace of infinity.
From here, from within, I release all limits,
all fears, and all smallness as I completely
trust this Infinite Wisdom.
It guides me always, guards me always,
and governs me all ways.
For all of my days.
Amen.

"At last the secret is out,
as it always must come in the end,
the delicious story is ripe to tell
an intimate friend; over teacups
and in the square the tongue has its desire;
still waters run deep, my dear,
there's never smoke without fire."

~ W.H. Auden ~

Tranquili-Tea

Be still and know God.
Be still and know God is all there is.
I claim in quiet, peaceful tranquility that
I am one with God.
My strength and satiation come from within.
I go there often to drink of the tranquil waters.
I am refreshed, replenished and rejuvenated.
From this place of purity and perfection,
I drink of my own goodness
and know my vessel will never empty.
I sip slowly and enjoy it totally.
My needs are satisfied, my desires realized.
I am all I need to be.
I am awakened and heightened.
No more, need I be frightened.
With each sip I am enlightened.
I am all I need to be.
Here, in tranquility, free from hostility and
perceived reality, I remember my divinity.
Thank you, Tranquil One. With my breath I let it be.
In the stillness God waits for me.
I allow this peaceful Force to set me free.
And so it does, and so it is, and so I am.
Amen.

"With each sip I taste the fire that gives its heat.
The water that gives its wetness.
The leaf that gives its spell.
The pot that gives its emptiness.
With each lingering sip
I cannot help but see all that makes tea,
as well, makes me."

~ The Minister of Leaves ~

Vitali-Tea

There is a vital force inside me
that is connected to something far greater.
It is an essential element that provides me
with unlimited strength.
This principle of life is God
and is truly all there is.
I am one with this Power,
this Force known as God.
I accept that this essential,
life-supporting phenomenon comes from
within me and works through me.
I am able to revitalize myself as often as necessary.
I need only sip of this ancient elixir
to remember my own good.
I give thanks for the potency
of the divine potential that exists in me and in all others.
Nothing real prevents this potent presence.
I release all that is perceived and allow for all that is possible.
For all is possible in God.
God is all that is possible in me.
So I let it be.
Amen.

Affirmation

I sip and I am soothed.
I heal and I am moved;
from this place to another.

Chapter Six

Choosing Tea for the Body

Affirmation

Part of me knows the history
and mystery of tea.
I drink while it is hot.
It finds the spot.

Choosing Tea for the Body

We are bombarded daily with all the things we should be doing for our bodies: the latest findings and contradictions, new afflictions and more addictions—via the television, the internet, new best-selling books, tabloid headlines, and infomercials. We are inundated with the hype about the latest miracle drugs, fail-safe diets, state-of-the-art exercise equipment and upcoming trends. They appear in our mail boxes, electronically and hand-delivered, and now, they are even on all the social networking sites. We are flooded non-stop and overwhelmed, are we not? Yes we are!

How about choosing the simple but tried-and-true tradition of "taking tea?" In many countries around the world, tea is used in ceremony and celebration, cherishing and honouring life and all that it entails. The United States is one of the few countries in the world where tea and its mystical and mythical properties have eluded us. Before we were even a country—we were avid tea drinkers. In 1773 upon taking a stand on the high taxes being charged on tea shipments, we ended our love for tea. We quickly became a coffee country and that has prevailed for more than two hundred years.

We are indeed a country where our accepted drug of choice is caffeine, as it is for most of the world. New "energy" drinks loaded with sugar, mystery herbs, minute amounts of the latest miracle berry and highly disguised caffeine are hitting the market and meeting with great success—mostly with a very young crowd. And yes, some even contain tea! In our quest to keep up, for peer approval, status and success, we are choosing other drugs as well. In our cities as well as small towns, in our heartlands, even in our schools, we are turning to drugs. We seem willing to try anything and everything to escape reality—or what we believe to be reality. Maybe that is the problem, we don't know what is real and perhaps we never have. It seems to be affecting so many: housewives, business executives, star athletes, soccer moms, movie stars, teenagers—the very fabric of our society is being compromised by the misuse of drugs.

People seem to be searching for something to fill a void so huge, to dull a pain so great, to cure a hunger so ravenous and to fill a need so deep that, for most, the problem defies explanation yet penetrates every fiber of their being. Could the problem be so great, so overwhelming, that it must be masked and drugged into submission? Or could it be something simple and pure and easy?

Let's say that it's the latter. Let's say that it is as simple and easy as preparing a cup of tea, sitting down with that steeped beverage, and connecting with a tradition enjoyed for thousands of years by billions of people. This could be oversimplifying the problem just a tad. But what if it's not? What if the tea leaves, rolled so tightly, locking in all their gifts, hold secrets waiting to be revealed? Perhaps the Chinese Emperor Shen Nung, also called "The Divine Healer," sensed something on another level as those first tea leaves shared their gifts and whispered their truths. Tea has been used for medicinal purposes since it was first discovered. It has long been known that keeping the body hydrated is crucial for healthy bodily functions. Drinking tea on a regular basis enhances fluid intake. Put most simply: hydrated cells are happy cells, and happy cells are healthy cells.

There is caffeine in tea naturally, although significantly less than in coffee; this moderate amount of caffeine does provide the body with a gentle lift and also stimulates the brain. People the world over have believed tea to have healing abilities, because when they drank it, they felt better.

Many unsubstantiated claims have been made about the benefits of tea to the body, but there may be more truth to them than we have recognized. While no one claims that tea is a cure-all, when consumed on a regular basis the flavonoids in tea do support the body in strengthening itself by supplying antioxidant properties. Certainly that is a worthy goal: to strengthen ourselves, from the inside out. That is what we are trying to accomplish here—on many levels.

Antioxidants serve to neutralize harmful molecules, (known as free radicals), that over time can damage cells and tissues and contribute to chronic diseases. When the cells of the body are nourished, they thrive, but when they are neglected and depleted, they begin to act strangely. In the case of certain types of cancer, (breast, lung, skin, stomach, digestive and urinary tract) research has shown that the flavonoids from tea inhibit some of the factors believed to increase cancer risk.

Flavonoids and other natural components in tea also have been found to help maintain a healthy cardiovascular system and a higher bone mineral density. The naturally occurring fluoride in tea inhibits the plaque-forming ability of oral bacteria, providing healthy tooth enamel and thus supporting good dental health.

The term "herbal teas" is actually a misnomer. Herbal teas are infusions of the leaves, roots, bark, seeds and/or flowers of various plants, but unless they contain the leaf of the Camellia sinensis plant, they really should not be referred to as "tea." Since there are many blends that contain both herbs as well as tea leaves, reading the list of ingredients for each blend is always suggested. Without the actual tea leaf, these herbal infusions, or "tisanes," lack the unique characteristics of tea and are not linked with the research on the potential health benefits of traditional teas. Although many herbal blends have wonderful, soothing abilities and offer various nutrients and health benefits, they are *not* tea.

Tea is an age-old beverage that has for millennia brought balance and harmony to spiritual rituals, celebrations and meditations. As a naturally contemplative beverage, it lends itself to any sort of ceremony that focuses on slowing down. Perhaps choosing to slow down for even a few moments a day will help bring us, individually, some inner peace. And perchance, when we start to feel better about ourselves, and begin our journey back to love, we will regard others in a kinder and gentler manner. These are the small steps that lead us toward a greater peace globally.

As the tea leaves unfurl and release their mysteries to a vessel of water, possibly in those quiet moments, life's secrets may just reveal themselves. In these precious moments of stillness, when all fear and worry dissolve, if only temporarily, we give ourselves the gift of reconnecting with something of immense power. Aligned with this power, we may experience clarity of mind, a body relieved of tension, a soul revisited and a heart open to love.

Is this not the absolute picture of perfection? And we can enjoy it every single day! We can acknowledge and celebrate these aspects of ourselves every day—and know that every facet of who we are deserves to be recognized and loved—the dark and the light.

The great mysteries expose themselves gently and with utter simplicity. To open ourselves to these mysteries, we first have to surrender to the concept that life does not have to be difficult, that life is meant to be celebrated and that every one of us deserves to be loved. The answers do come, one whisper at a time, one sip at a time, but only when we make ourselves available to them and open to the power of love.

Take time for tea. Make time to do something healing, nurturing and loving for the body on a daily basis. Remember to start slowly and become adjusted to the new routines, knowing that this is all of our own choosing. We create the quality of the love in our lives one choice at a time, one cup at a time, and one sip at a time.

Affirmation

I make time for tea.
I take time for me.
I am in harmony.

"I invite you magnanimously to please be my guest
for tea at a room with high standards of taste
where the hostess remembers my face,
and greets me by name at the door
and recalls what I've ordered before,
and inquires kindly after my day,
and appreciates all that I say.
Shall have orange pekoe for the pot and Darjeeling,
as likely as not, or if you are not in the pink
our hostess knows which herbs to drink,
like ginger to help with the grippe
mixed with cinnamon and the rosehip;
or fresh lemon balm if you wish,
perhaps blended with sweet licorice.
So whether you feel well or ill,
this refreshment will quite fit the bill and, of course,
you will quite enjoy me.
Yours truly. R.S.V.P."

~ Aubrey Henslow ~

Liber-Tea

I remove all restraints. I set myself free.
This is emancipation day and I claim my liberty.
God is all I see; God is all there is.
Freedom opens me to see that we have always been one.
I no longer hold myself prisoner.
No one or no thing holds me captive.
For the first time I see that I am good;
good enough, just as I am.
The blindfold and shackles have been removed.
Unchained, unconfined, and finally, I am unconstrained.
I see God's pure light and my own bright light.
In jubilation and celebration I give thanks.
I am grateful for this divine liberation.
My soul is free; there is no intervention.
Relieved of ties, tears and tension, I soar freely.
I live wholly, and I am complete.
I rise up, I wise up; there is no defeat.
I go within and never go without.
In love I am healed; with grace I am free.
All is assured. There is no place for doubt.
I claim my freedom now.
I live it, and so it is.
Amen.

"Tea; the drink declared to be most wholesome, preserving in perfect health until extreme old age. It maketh the body active and lusty. It helpeth the headache, giddiness and heaviness thereof."

~ Tomas Garway ~ Advertisement 1658

Sobrie-Tea

I am free to feel and free to be.
I celebrate my sobriety.
In my cleared state, I can feel God.
God is the Power. God is all there is.
I now see that the Higher Power is in me.
One in this Power, one with this Presence,
I bring myself into divine alignment.
Feelings intact, no fear of attack, I see
myself for who I truly am.
I am strong, confident and worthy of love.
I abstain from negation.
I remain in celebration.
I gain concentration. I claim jubilation.
I stay focused; I stay real; I stay here.
Here I know my goodness and
here I know my God-ness.
I am clean, clear, guilt free and shame free.
God lives through me.
I cannot miss the opportunity to live each day,
one day at a time, to be in joy and to be in the now.
I release all else and claim only good.
I cannot be forsaken or misunderstood.
I claim my good now.
I own it, I live it, and so it is.
Amen.

"Tea's proper use is to amuse the idle,
and relax the studious,
and dilute the full meals of
those who cannot use exercise,
and will not use abstinence."

~ Samuel Johnson ~

Longevi-Tea

This is my life to live.
I choose to live it to the fullest—to the greatest
and to the highest.
I embrace all that is, with all my ability.
I choose God because God is all there is.
And in pure divine health, I claim longevity.
One with God, vim, vigour and vitality,
my body finds the peace of wholeness.
And in this oneness, all dis-ease,
all dis-function and dis-repair
in the physical is blessed by the Divine
and is now healed.
My temple is sacred and sanctified.
All good comes to me and
I know only good health.
For this divine restoration,
I claim jubilation and sincere appreciation.
I release worry and fear and fretting.
With God's grace, I'll not be forgetting
that I am whole, healed, healthy and happy.
My word makes it so, and so it is.
Amen.

Affirmation

My heart beats at a whole new pace.
With love, I am in a state of grace.

Chapter Seven

Choosing Love for the Heart

Affirmation

Like a rose, my heart unfolds.
Beauty is all it knows.

Choosing Love for the Heart

We hear so much about the mind-body-soul connection, but where does the heart enter into this equation? We are very familiar with this triad, this is true, but when the heart is added to this expression, there is completion. It seems that if the heart isn't in something, then the "thing" is not quite complete.

When we speak of the soul, we often gesture toward the heart, as though that is where the soul lives, somewhere deep in the heart area. Perhaps it does, perhaps we'll never know, and maybe it doesn't even matter.

The heart has always seemed like a very special place. We could suppose that God lives there, if God and the soul are really one and the same. We use phrases such as, *in my heart of hearts* or *from the bottom of my heart*, which seem to point to an exceptional place. God could live there. *I felt it with all my heart* suggests that God had a part in it. *The core of my being* makes us think of the heart area, given that "core" usually refers to the center or heart of something. Yes, the heart does indeed seem like a powerful place.

Falling in love, being in love, is always associated with the heart. We draw hearts to symbolize love. A heart has even replaced the word "love" on bumper stickers and T-shirts. We just automatically know what the heart symbol stands for.

If someone has *put their heart* into something, we know that thing is special right from the start. If someone *has put their heart and soul* into something, then we know not much could be left out. On the other hand, if someone does something *half-heartedly*, we can be sure not much effort was put forth and that something of significance is missing.

Heart and soul have sometimes seemed interchangeable, yet we seem to know instinctively that there is a subtle difference. If someone is said to have a lot of soul, that's a little different from someone with a lot of heart. They are not the same, and yet very close. Surely that is no coincidence. We are often asked, *what does your heart tell you*? Or we're told, *go with your heart* or *trust your heart*. Then we've heard, *what does your head tell you*? As if head and heart are two distinct realms. Physically they may be, but metaphysically they are not.

It has been said that the journey from the head to the heart is the longest we'll ever take. Does that mean we have drawn a line somewhere separating the two? Why would we have done that? We learned somewhere along the way to live in the mind, the lower mind that is. This would probably be when the difficulties started.

In matters of great importance, we rarely hear or say, *just trust your head*. Rather, *trust your heart* usually applies in such matters. *Trust your head* sounds somewhat brutal and lacking in compassion. When it comes to business matters or day-to-day dealings, we try desperately to leave our hearts out of the picture. How wonderful it would be to have businesses with heart! A few do exist, and perhaps there is a trend toward more of these businesses, but the bottom line often dictates how much heart is allowed. As soon as money is involved, something changes. If we are business managers, we are often trained to leave our hearts out and deal only with the logical head aspects. We are taught not to get personal, not to *take things to heart*.

How on earth (and only on earth) do we leave our hearts out of anything we do?

Could that be why the journey from head to heart appears to be so difficult? It is not difficult though; we do have the ability to live with fully loving and trusting hearts.

So here we have this physical heart of ours, protected so ingeniously by the rib cage, beating away, pumping blood, energizing and purifying with every beat. How can we possibly ignore it? What about the statistics of heart disease and heart attacks? We hear on a regular basis that heart problems are increasing. We are walking around with hearts in dis-ease as the word clearly indicates. Heart disease is currently the number one killer of women. Now what kind of message is that sending?

Could it be that because we are ignoring our hearts, they are crying out for attention—emotionally, spiritually and now, physically? If we were more familiar with the concept of loving ourselves, perhaps our hearts would be more at ease and would be satisfied. Feeling unworthy and impure has led us down a dark path, and in the shadows we have taken up behaviours that are self-destructive and self-defeating. Low self-esteem and little self-love are big problems that need to be addressed at a higher and deeper level.

How do we choose love for the heart? First by choosing love for ourselves, by believing we have done nothing that has separated us from God. We are worthy of God's unconditional love and deserving of a life that is whole and good and with purpose. We then learn to love others as we love ourselves, and not just when they agree with us or are like us. We can express love every opportunity we get, even if it is as simple as a smile or a nod of the head. And we are all capable of that! This is also about standing in front of the mirror and declaring love to and for ourselves. When we look into our own eyes and see beyond all our past perceived imperfections, our beauty and magnificence become abundantly clear. Perhaps not immediately but isn't it worth trying? This is the greatest gift we can give back to God— to love ourselves—to raise our own image of ourselves, our self-esteem, our own self-worth and to find our bliss.

Expressing love at every opportunity we can is not about physical love; this is about love that can transcend barriers and borders. We can even love someone who does not want to be loved; the love is received on another level if the human element cannot receive it. Souls have their way of communicating, and all they really know is love, because they come from God; and God Is Love.

Could it all be as simple as the Beatles claimed? "Love Is All We Need." YES! YES! YES!

How many times have those lyrics been sung by our very own lips—words that the conscious mind could not even comprehend? Repeat these words and simply allow them to resonate with the soul, the mind, the body and, of course, with the heart. *Love is all we need.* We can choose to open our hearts and let love into our lives, into every aspect of our lives. We can indeed say *YES* to love because we have the capability to choose love over anything and everything else.

What does my heart say? Ask this question and listen closely, remaining still and silent—although when the heart speaks, it speaks loudly and clearly; we are just used to drowning it out. It has also been said that we use only about ten percent of our brain's capability. How much of our heart's ability are we really using? How many times in a single day could we have expressed more love or contributed more love—whether it's to our so-called loved ones or to someone in the outside world?

How often has it actually seemed easier to be kinder to a stranger than to someone we claim to love? In just considering these questions, we open ourselves to all we are capable of in so many ways. Why do we hold back? What are we waiting for? Let's start now by opening up to the love of God.

When someone is kind enough and open enough to give us their heart, in love, we want to remember to treat this as the special gift it is. Most of us know the feeling of a broken heart. Some of us have had limited experiences with it; others have limited themselves for a lifetime because of it. Let's not take lightly a heart given out of love. Let's cherish that gift, nurture it, and if it cannot be returned, then please be gentle. Know that no love is ever wasted, even if it is never tasted. Never be afraid to express love, for in expressing love we reveal our true selves, our God-selves. Express it in all its endless forms—through art, music, dance, poetry—the list goes on forever just as God's love for us is never-ending. Express it in the mirror to a child of God who needs it and is longing for it and who truly does deserve it, YOU.

Metaphysically, there are energy centers in the body known as chakras. The heart chakra is centrally located; three chakras are above it and three are below. This is a powerful area of the body, physically and spiritually. It is usually associated with the colour green, which is stimulating to the heart chakra and the body in general. Seeing the physical heart in a warm and soothing green light during those moments of stillness and oneness is very healing and invigorating for the heart. To repeat again, the statement, *Love is all I need*, can add such depth to this moment of communion, this moment of celebration. It allows for the opening of the heart to the love within and to all the love in the universe, which is God's love in totality.

If a heart has been shut down for some time, which is to say, has been functioning far below its capability to love, it may need a gentle jump-start. Using the power of the mind in meditation to envision the opening of the heart is extremely potent, even though it may need to be practiced frequently. If there has been a figurative padlock on the heart, visualize it springing open. See a door to the heart opening and then enter: watch what happens.

It's important to put our heart into everything we do, and as much of our heart as we can. The heart is such a vital part of the human body, as it is to the human experience. It is far more than simply an organ, a muscle, or a pump, it has an intelligence all of its own and is our connection to the entire universe and every one in it.

Following the heart will surely lead us down the path of love. A heart that knows God can only know love. Knowing God and expressing our God-selves is love in its purest form, and this now opens what is referred to as the *Sacred Heart*. This is where the love came from that Jesus the Christ, exuded and taught. When we open to love and celebrate our spiritual heart as well as our physical heart, and truly listen to the beat, we can feel a definite rhythm. And this is the rhythm of God's universe.

"Now stir the fire, and close the shutters fast,
let fall the curtains, wheel the sofa around.
And while the bubbling and loud-hissing urn
throws up a steamy column,
and the cups that cheer but not inebriate,
wait on each,
so let us welcome peaceful evening in."

~ William Cowper ~

Eterni-Tea

God has no beginning and no end.
God is the All.
God is all there is, ever was, and ever will be.
God's love has no end;
it is everlasting, timeless, and without interruption.
I was conceived from this love.
In God's love and truth there is no deterioration or corruption.
From this oneness I claim all my goodness.
All good comes to me easily and
flows from me freely and I have perpetuity.
My goodness knows no time or space,
no boundaries, no limits do I face.
Eternity is home; it is my birthplace—and there I will return.
I can go there briefly with clarity of mind
and with an open heart.
Joy and bliss are what I always find.
So grateful am I; on the wings of love do I fly.
I release all concerns and fears, all constraints and tears.
I send thanks to the Ever-Living
whose love is unfading, unfailing and always forgiving.
So it is now, as it was then, and, will be forever.
Amen.

"Tea! Thou soft, thou sober, sage,
and venerable liquid . . .
thou female tongue-running, smile-smoothing,
heart-opening, wind-tippling cordial,
to whose glorious insipidity
I owe the happiest moment of my life,
let me fall prostrate."

~ Colley Cibber ~

Mediocri-Tea

I do not have to settle for less.
I choose a life that is full and complete,
with no more stress.
I am at the place where the middle ground
and the high ground meet.
I close my eyes and open my heart.
I am ready for a brand new start.
From here, I know God is all there is
and we are one and I release inferiority.
I feel my spirit rise as I embark on a fresh, lush path.
The rocks and burrs are still there—
they no longer slow me down.
I am stronger and more confident.
I now know my own good, and worthiness, and,
I see it in everyone else.
For this gift of seeing good, knowing truth,
and living well, I give sincere thanks.
In the grace of good, love is understood.
Love is all there is; love is all I need.
Everything else I ask God to take away
and in the light of a new day,
I am shown another way and I never settle for less.
I let go, I go in.
I release and let God begin.
And so It does.
Amen.

"Attune your hearts to the other guests.
This final "secret" teaching,
the desirability of harmonious behavior,
applies both to host and guests.
The realization hints at another truth of tea;
it takes just as much discipline and practice
to learn how to receive as well
as it does to know how to give well."

~ Rikyu ~ "Seven Secrets of Tea"

Synchronici-Tea

In this world, this cosmos, this universe,
God is all there is.
God came first—a plan, an arrangement,
an agreement, all settled upon.
Everything in perfect order, in precise harmony,
all events and all beings together in divine synchronicity.
No accidents, no coincidence, no blunders and no omissions.
All have a purpose; all have their missions—aware or unaware,
asleep or awake.
I realize the magnificence of all it takes.
I accept and appreciate my own attributes;
my good, my abilities, and my place in this plan.
I embody these qualities and give thanks every chance I can.
My heart and eyes are open to the divine events all
around me and from within me.
Heaven is right here, right where I am.
Like a beautifully choreographed waltz;
life is a dance in perfect rhythm with God's master plan.
I succumb only to the Divine Maestro.
As a vital part of the orchestra,
I play in perfect harmony with all there is and
where all coincide.
For all that is so,
I find inside.
Amen.

Affirmation

In releasing, I am relieved.
In forgiving, I am forgiven.

Chapter Eight

Forgiveness
The Key

Affirmation

To forgive—Divine.
To forget—Divine.
To move on—Divine.
To live on—Divine.

Forgiveness—The Key

All that has been written and read is fine and good, but if we have no place for the information, it gets lost and thus serves little purpose. This amazing brain of ours has often been likened to a computer. Information goes in, it is filed, and then it is retrieved when needed. Yet we have all had times when we could not find that information anywhere. During that exam, we know we know the answer, but where did it go? It appears to be forgotten, lost or misplaced. The quote we thought we would never forget—it was so profound—gone. The name of the person we just shook hands with—poof!

The brain and the mind are not the same thing. We've been told that we only use a small percentage of our brains. That probably applies to the mind as well, perhaps even more so. This seems to be a reoccurring pattern—not using all we've been blessed with.

The mind is assuredly one way to connect with God, so therefore it must be unlimited. The heart, soul and mind have all got to be connected to God. Is it not a clear channel between those three that bring us peace of mind? That harmony, that serenity, that euphoria we are all yearning to experience—surely that cannot come from an outside source; it has to come from within. But we must clear the way.

Most of us are walking around overloaded, shifting from overdrive to burnout. There seems to be too much of everything, yet not enough of what is vital. Our systems are about to crash; there's no memory space left available. We hang in there, though, processing slowly, getting impatient and frustrated, about to melt down completely. This cannot be the way to live. Not wholly and completely—not at all.

To clear a path for bliss, we have to go back to the mainframe. Is there a lot of old stuff stored in there that is no longer needed? Can some things be deleted: old beliefs, haunting memories, limited goals, thoughts of lack, "shameful" secrets, and wounds yet unhealed? These are the things that are taking up space, valuable room that could be used for something else, something good and positive, something like self-love. These are the things that overwhelm and overload us. Like most people with their computers, the good stuff is seldom backed up, but those negative thoughts have backups for the backups! Instead of deleting them, we keep bringing up these same old files, replaying them, reliving them, over and over again. It's now time to hit the delete key.

Forgiveness is that key. It is the switch that allows us to interface with the God Force in our lives. But here is where we ask ourselves, w*hat version of God am I currently running?* If we are operating with an outdated interpretation, say, from the time we were six or sixteen, then it is time to upgrade. There are many wonderful, enlightened teachings out there that provide insight and shed a new light on what we have been missing. What *new* version of God feels better? "Seek and you will find." There it is again. And one more time, what we desire is not *out there*. These interpretations are merely tools that can assist us in connecting with who we are and what God truly is, and thus, open to our own innate spiritual wisdom. In allowing the pure power of the Master Processor to source our systems, there will be no more power failures and power surges will then be a good thing. It is this God Force, the Holy Spirit, the All, the Presence, the Divine—calling It whatever we are comfortable with—that does the healing. This Power Source has the answers to our questions and the solutions to our problems. We may never understand just how things work, but it is in the trusting of this Divine Wisdom that we are given the space, cleared of our clutter and relieved of our self-inflicted burdens.

We must forgive everyone and anyone we feel has wronged us, hurt us, limited us or stopped us dead in our tracks. The true reality behind forgiving everyone is that we end up forgiving *ourselves*.

The unwillingness to forgive ourselves gives rise to the guilt, shame and confusion that plague us. This is what keeps us in a place of low self-esteem and blocks out most of our capacity to love ourselves. Because in actuality, no one can make us feel these things unless we allow it, so in forgiving them, we are absolving ourselves for allowing those emotions to limit us and keep us from truly loving ourselves. From forgiveness comes freedom. We forgive as a gift to ourselves, not to the other person. Most often the other person has no idea of the pain we have felt by their actions. That is why we need to forgive ourselves, first and foremost, so we can then move into self-love and experience true BLISS.

Anger, vengeance and hatred keep us prisoners of our own lower minds. They simply take up too much space and need to be erased completely. God provides this clearing service free of charge—just for our willingness to forgive and the steps we take at every level to release these negative energies. The added benefits of forgiveness include a greatly expanded capacity to love ourselves and others, to learn easily and to live effortlessly. Because, truly, if we aren't forgiving, then we aren't living!

If we are not living the life we came here to live, not living up to our full potential and not loving potently, we will never know BLISS; this results in a life with no joy. A life that lacks joy and happiness is a life separate from God and a life in the shadows. In the light of forgiveness, there is room to grow, to reach out, to open and reveal all the gifts with which we were born.

Only by believing we are separate from God could any dark presence ever be alive within us. It is from not forgiving ourselves for our negative thoughts, for our careless wanderings into revenge and for limiting love that we shrink back from the light. God is all there is; anything else, we have just made up!

Forgiveness is self-exorcism. Those hindering thoughts are the conjured demons that keep us from a life of joy and a life filled with love. That is why it is so important that we start now and continue until we have removed all vestiges of human limitation, so that the heart and mind are allowed to return to their original default setting of *open*.

A heart that does not know forgiveness has shriveled and closed tightly over a wound or multiple wounds. It is a heart with a padlock on it—still pumping, still beating, still trying—but has emotionally and spiritually, been locked. So here we have this being, still a child of God, with a heart closed to love and self-love, a mind in overload about to crash at any moment, stumbling through a falsely-perceived difficult existence. This is no way to live. And in no way will we ever be able to honour or fulfill our true purpose with this impediment.

We are hard-wired with a capacity we have yet to exceed. God has installed a hard drive—a mind—of infinite ability, yet most of us think our systems are antiquated and inadequate. This translates to, *I'm too old, I'm not smart enough, poor me*. We can get past this limiting self-talk simply by opening to the concept of releasing. We must let go of every small thought we ever had about ourselves and move into the illuminated place of self-love. We pardon our own memory lapses—the times we forgot to remember who we are. We forgive the judgements we have of others, as well as those we have of ourselves.

Forgiveness allows for optimum performance. Our systems reboot themselves in those quiet moments of meditation, prayer and contemplation. A simple cup of tea can get our systems whirling again at peak levels. For in our moments of stillness and forgiveness, we enter into a conscious oneness with the Source of limitlessness, the Source of infinite, ancient wisdom.

The wisdom of the ages is not found hidden in caves or on remote mountaintops. The Truth is within us. When we understand this, we summon the courage to ask those profound questions that previously we only allowed ourselves to ponder occasionally because we thought we could not comprehend the answers. But God has no secret agendas and no hidden messages. So why not ask: *What is the meaning of my life? What is my purpose and what am I passionate about? How can I make a difference? Who am I and who do I choose to be? What will I do with my life?* The list is endless, but the guarantee is that the answers will not come in a booming voice from up in the sky.

We think we are seeking the answers but the answers are seeking us.

The answers will come one whisper at a time, which is why moments of quiet and stillness are so vital to the very fabric of who we are. The answers will come from within. This is where God is. How many times do we have to hear "The Kingdom of Heaven is within" before we get it? Oh, that's right; we have no more space available to receive these messages. So before we ask these questions, we must provide room to hear the answers. This we do by forgiving and releasing all the clutter that has backed up our systems. With all these thoughts and beliefs excised, we make space for God; we give our minds back over to God. We offer our hearts as pristine accommodations of five-star quality. Simply by forgiving, we come back into the light, and by the grace of God, we open to the joy of living a full and loving life.

Forgiveness opens all the channels. Just think of all that extra room for the mind to tap into the Holy Spirit, to actually hear God. Now think of the heart, a heart with no boundaries, no shackles; a heart free to love; one open to forgiving and opening through forgiveness. A heart, soul and mind all joined as a conduit for God in our very own human body—perfection at its finest. The process of forgiveness is forever ongoing. As we grow spiritually, we reach new levels of understanding, about ourselves and about others. As we mature spiritually, we extend and expand to places of contentment, and we can experience some very profound moments of clarity, moments when we just know that we know. This is when we are able to forgive from another place, another level. From this new vantage point, there is a release, an understanding, and true inner peace.

These places and these levels are a state of consciousness, ascension from the lower mind into the higher mind. A clearing of the lower mind provides the space and allows the wisdom of the God Force to come through with more than just words. All this Force knows is love, so the sense of peace and contentment that comes with it—is love.

The de-fragmentation process we simply trust and turn over to God. We are all one with the One Mind; we all share this Mind. This is why peace of mind is such a cherished gift. If we are all sharing a mind of chaos, we will never experience BLISS, nor will this planet ever know peace.

God has plenty to give us in place of the endless mind-chatter of self-doubt. But we have to make room to receive. We can consciously choose to give God space, or we can instead pass up the gift and hold on forever to our precious *junk*.

Forgiving is a choice. We can choose to forgive any time we desire. We pray and make this choice; we meditate and make this choice; we sip tea and make this choice. And by making the choice, we live a loving life that is full, whole and complete, and this is true BLISS, and how we live a life in constant celebration of the Divine.

Affirmation

Every day I learn more about me.
Every way I learn to love more of me.

"If a man has no tea in him, he is incapable of understanding truth and beauty."

~ Japanese Proverb ~

Chari-Tea

I start by being charitable to myself.
In loving kindness, I realize the validity
of my purpose; my reason for being here.
By reaching out to assist others I help myself.
We are all one in God, and God
is all there is. By being compassionate
and considerate of others, I learn to be gentler with myself.
I choose to no longer see any shortcomings.
I think more mild and merciful thoughts.
This allows me to see my own good and my own
God-like qualities.
Divine charity starts with me.
I have plenty to give and by giving, I open to receive.
I give thanks to the Benevolent Giver.
I am always accepted for the growing spirit I am.
With Spirit growing in me,
I learn to give and forgive.
I learn to live and let live.
It is all good because it is all God.
It is God's kindness and generosity and charity to me
that never ceases.
I let go of all other thoughts, and trust the One Mind,
the One Thought that started it all.
Amen.

"Tea is wealth itself, because there is nothing
that cannot be lost, no problem that will not disappear,
no burden that will not float away, between the
first sip and the last."

~ The Minister of Leaves ~

Responsibili-Tea

I take it easy. I keep things simple.
I break it down to what is really significant.
God matters; I matter. God is love; love matters.
I am one with God and we are all one.
Everything else that fills my life is just clutter.
I prioritize; I sort out.
I can be trusted to do a good job.
I don't have to say "yes" to everything,
but I say "yes" to the Ever-Thing, and I say "yes" to me.
I lovingly take on the responsibility of living in accountability.
What I think, say, and do, I become; therefore,
I think good thoughts, speak good words, and do good work.
I am good. I am from God—good is all I can be.
For the divine trust put in me, I give thanks.
To those who love and believe in me, I am grateful and faithful.
I am clutter-free; nothing blocks or hinders me.
I release having to be everything to everyone
and trust it all over to the One—the forever living One,
the forever loving One.
Amen.

"Tea had come as a deliverer to a land that called
for deliverance; a land of beef and ale,
of heavy eating and abundant drunkenness;
of gray skies and harsh winds;
of strong-nerved, stout-purposed,
slow-thinking men and women.
Above all, a land of sheltered homes
and warm firesides
that were waiting—waiting for the bubbling kettle
and the fragrant breath of tea."

~ Agnes Reppiler ~

Simplici-Tea

Love is simple, easy and it comes to me freely,
without complexity.
I clear my life; I simplify and remember
God is all there is and that we are one.
The material world becomes much lighter.
My future now appears brighter.
In the illumination of this simplicity,
I see my own goodness and my own Godliness.
Ostentation, formality, extravagance and difficulty disappear.
My life is simple, loving is natural, being is easy. I am free.
I choose liberty and I live purely.
With grace I live in divine simplicity.
God comes through me easily.
Nothing blocks my receptivity.
I receive all I need from the Divine Giver.
I give back my thanks and appreciation
and know gratitude from a whole new place.
I have made room for God.
I have saved some space.
I allow God in and I allow God out.
It all flows easily and simply as I let it be.
Amen.

Affirmation

I am opening, I am unfurling,
I am surrendering . . . I am.

Chapter Nine

The Agony of the Leaves

Affirmation

No more agony,
no more anxiety,
there is only Divinity surrounding me.

The Agony of the Leaves

Tea masters and tea tasters have a phrase for the process that the tea leaves undergo as they are immersed in boiling water. This process is referred to as "the agony of the leaves," because it is said that the leaves actually appear to be "agonizing" over giving up their treasured gifts.

The tea leaves unfurling and unfolding as they steep is truly a dance the leaves do as they expose themselves in and to the hot water. All the flavour that was locked securely in the leaves as they were dried and rolled, all the aroma that was sealed in, and all the secrets that have been tightly held—all these—are being released into the freshly-boiled water. Their only purpose up until this moment of culmination has been to guard and keep their oils and flavours safely preserved.

The time must be right and the conditions precise for a total infusion and explosion of all the cherished possessions sealed within each and every leaf. What was mere water, albeit a necessity of life; becomes totally transformed; containing the additional life-enhancing, as well as spirit-enhancing properties.

Tea is a beverage unlike any other, offering tranquility and balance with each and every sip. Its liquor sustains precious moments of reflection and contemplation, a fluid that can rejuvenate a parched and desolate soul. Once steeped, it pleads to be savoured until the last pot and the very last drop. It is a steamy hot liquid that has been revered and shared by royals and peasants alike for thousands of years.

All of this and more is in every cup of tea.

Are we ourselves not unlike the tea leaf, with our gifts and mysteries locked tightly within us? And like the leaves, do we not need something that unlocks us and opens us to our true potential?

We all have talents and abilities. These are gifts we came with, and the keys to the kingdom are ours for the asking. As life presents the opportunities—the keys—we are given the choice to accept or reject them. These are the chances given to us to unfurl ourselves completely. Every day holds the potential and countless opportunities for us to express who we are. Do we express or repress? A leaf that never opens completely takes its potential to the trash, never to be revealed or released. Is it possible that we could go to the grave with our potential, with our dream, with our purpose, still locked inside of us?

Perhaps there are times of real agony in our lives, times when we are doubled over, agonizing over what appears to be a painful existence. But in those moments, we can choose to remember to surrender to the water—to release it all over to God. Surrendering allows us to open and to expose our gifts. Through surrender, we step out of what we incorrectly refer to as our "comfort zone," which in reality provides us with little comfort at all. This is the zone that says, *I can't* or *I'm not ready yet*. Well, it's time to "give it up," as they say. Give up living half a life, give up settling for less, and give up mediocrity and all pettiness. For most of us, this list could get quite long, but by letting go and forgiving and ceasing the negative thinking, the list itself will shrink.

Agony is needless suffering. Whether the struggle is with the mind, the heart or the body, there is no need to prolong this struggle. What follows surrender is the release from agony. The relinquishment of all burdens grants permission for a resurrection, so that the mind can be restored, the heart revived, the body renewed and the soul reconnected. The resurrection is a reawakening.

A familiar picture comes to mind with the word *agony*. Many artists over the centuries have painted their version of what is referred to as, "The Agony in the Garden." Jesus is depicted as forlorn and usually kneeling over a large rock in complete despair and surrender. He knows the crucifixion is imminent. His three disciples have fallen asleep—it is only he and God. He surrenders his will, he utters the phrase "Thy will be done," and an angel is said to appear to provide him comfort. Jesus knew he could not be abandoned, not by God, not ever. No matter how it appeared in those tender moments in the Garden of Gethsemane, he knew he was not alone. He is said to have alerted his disciples to "not enter into temptation"—the temptation to misperceive, to misjudge and to mislead.

The temptation to give in to anger and revenge is alive in all of us; these are the trappings of the lower mind, an easily-led-astray lower mind. Some very holy and profound moments come forth from our times of agony. These moments are precious teaching tools that we can accept or reject, but first we have to be aware enough to see beyond the agony. Jesus was eminently above the restrictions of the lower mind and was already well into the forgiving of his killers long before the crucifixion transpired. That is love in its highest and truest form. His purpose had been served.

Have we received his message accurately?

Once the tea leaves have given up their precious cargo, all that remains is the dance; the dance of freedom. The leaves now move about the water freely, confidently knowing that they have fulfilled their mission. Their purpose has been satisfied. They have completely transformed the water and turned it into something delightful for someone else to enjoy. How enlightened is that?

There is a little secret left though. Those tea leaves, now completely unfurled, still have life left in them. Most leaves can do another dance, and several types of teas have numerous infusions in one lifetime. To continue the metaphor, once we've "done it"—lived through the agonizing times, it's not over; there is still life left, still precious cargo within us all—love survives all our tragedies. We have numerous opportunities for renaissance, for unlimited rebirths; because unlike the mighty tea leaf, we can tap into the true Source and regenerate ourselves with love again and again.

We do this in whatever manner best suits each individual. We can do it with tea and prayer and meditation, and we do it with love. If there is no love behind the motivation, we are just stirring an empty cup. We fill up the cup every chance we get because we know the Source is limitless. What are we putting in the cup? SELF LOVE. And we are the cups, the vessels for God. Can it be that the treasured Holy Grail, if it is indeed a chalice, is within us? Could it be that each and every one of us contains the answers to the secrets and the mysteries for which we have long been searching? We'll never know if we cannot open up enough to unveil them. No one should go to the grave with a dance or a dream still in them. None of us are "spent" after just one infusion. When we think that there is nothing left inside, that we have dried up or it's just not worth the effort, or that the agony is far too great, bring to mind (and heart) the picture of Jesus in surrender at the rock, in his garden of agony.

Many great teachers from all religions have walked this earth to teach us love—love for ourselves and for each other. In loving ourselves, we are able and willing to think again, to choose again, and to try again. Life is too precious to live it only partially and too magnificent to remain mundane. We must get over the agony to dance freely. Instead of locking up and doubling over, we can open our arms and our hearts and surrender our minds to God. The tea leaf, in its simplicity and humility, has the power to transform water just as each and every one of us has the potential to transform ourselves, and then, to transform the world.

We may never again look at a cup of tea or tea leaves in the same manner as before. Some have never looked at all. This is a challenge to "take up the cup" in celebration. To open up and unlock all that dwells within; to wake up the sleeping giant of wisdom, and step out of the shadows; to break up the frozen force of infinite power; to love and forgive ourselves; to trust God, to know God, and to know GOD is all there is. LOVE is all there is.

Affirmation

I sip tea and I celebrate me.
I release all I can be.

"There is no trouble so great or grave
that cannot be much diminished by
a nice cup of tea."

~ Bernard-Paul Heroux ~

Securi-Tea

The surety of God provides me with the security of God.
God is all there is and all the protection I need.
With this Presence, I am safe;
with this Power, I am whole, and we are one.
I am certain in God; this is God's guarantee.
This makes us one for all eternity.
A divine promise whispered to me
one day while sipping hot tea.
One sip at a time—inner peace came to me.
I am now free from all agony and fear.
I am secure in my being
and confident in my good.
My future is assured, insured and secured.
I am grateful for the gift of this word.
I am safe and guarded by this holy shield.
I rest in this certainty, this divine security,
and trust it all over to God.
When I do, I know no danger, and no stranger,
we are all one when we surrender to the Real One.
In this surety there is purity and power; grace and growth;
faith and hope, and divine love far beyond the human scope.
It is there for me and I am there for it.
And this keeps me safe.
Amen.

"A toast to the grace of the pot, ready at all times
to give up its emptiness for the tea."

~ The Minister of Leaves ~

Difficul-Tea

No struggle, no strife;
no impracticability, no impossibility.
I believe in God and I believe in me.
I remember that God is all there is and
difficulty no longer exists.
I surrender—I become one with all there is.
I accept and I allow.
I embody, I embrace; all complexity I erase.
I move ahead freely; I can see clearly.
What is there really?—Only God.
All outcomes are good, feasible and obtainable.
I am grateful and thankful, productive and proactive.
I know the difference between diffidence and confidence;
the difference between confinement and detachment.
I release all fears and struggles back over to God
and know no boundaries, no confines.
All is fair and all is fine in the hands of the Divine.
I let go and let God.
All is easy and effortless for in surrender
there is simplicity.
And without perplexity
there is bliss.
Amen.

"While there's tea, there's hope."

~ Sir Arthur Pinero ~

Anxie-Tea

I reach into the purest part of me
and know my future is secure.
I have nothing to fear, God is so near.
All outcomes are clear.
I close out everything and see the Ever-Thing.
God is all I see. God is all there is.
Agony and apprehension are abolished.
I am one again with the One, again and forever.
In the absence of anxiety I am absolute.
The Absolute I Am assures anchorage in a harbour
of security and prosperity;
a home free of all adversity,
an asylum from worry and fret,
a shelter from aggression and obsession,
as well as a sanctuary from uncertainty and instability.
In God I am safe and good, and I find my refuge.
For this I am eternally grateful and thankful.
I release the anxiety, the anguish and agony.
I allow God stewardship; God becomes my guide.
My vessel sails freely from this day forward.
It is safe, and so am I, and it is so.
Amen.

Affirmation

I find a new way
but it's an old way,
it's God's way, and now my way.

Chapter Ten

A New "Way of Tea"

Affirmation

I bless all that has been
and welcome the unseen.

A New "Way of Tea"

Many countries, including China, Korea, Russia and Great Britain, have been widely known for the varied ceremonies and celebrations they have created around the serving of tea. But nowhere has the ritual been carried out with more formality and intricacy than in Japan.

The Japanese tea ceremony, or cha-no-yu, is considered an art form. There are many art forms, or "ways," studied in Japan. It is through the tea ceremony that the "way of tea," or chado, is learned and perfected. This ritual has been taught, studied and performed for centuries.

Most North Americans have heard of the Japanese tea ceremony, but few understand what it is really all about. It is a very precise and detailed event. For most lay people observing the ritual, it appears quite simple, and one might wonder what all the fuss is about. But the skilled eye can see beyond the physical into the spiritual aspects of the presentation. In our everyday haste, many of us would find the thought of a ceremony that can last as long as four hours to be too much. There is a resurgence of tea happening quietly in North America. We might even call it a resurrection. What died an untimely death in 1773 is slowly coming back to life, and tea is capturing the attention of a growing number of people seeking alternatives to and from the "rat race." Tea seems to be a common thread that entwines humans with peace of mind.

Much is involved in the "way of tea," and attempting to describe all the aspects of the ceremony would be too cumbersome. What is most significant about the ritual is that it teaches us to live in the moment and to be aware of everything: aesthetically, intellectually, physically and spiritually. To achieve this, the guests and the host/hostess focus their senses with great intensity. No mundane, earthly thoughts are allowed to disturb or distract the participants from their goal of remaining totally present in the occasion, and to the activities at hand.

The host/hostess is taught by a teacher, and sometimes it takes decades to master all the procedures. One learns grace, patience, selflessness and attentiveness to the needs of others. The senses are fine-tuned; the movements are delicate and are learned not with the brain but with the body. The unfurling of self-realization and an ever-deepening presence of mind leads to a mastery of life that every tea teacher strives to edify in each student.

During the ceremony, talking is minimal, and when it occurs, it is only in appreciation of the handcrafted items used in the ceremony, including: the floral arrangements, the calligraphy, the teapots, tea bowls and other utensils. When participants and observers open their eyes and hearts to see the ceremony for all its treasures, the spiritual aspects become very clear. The water, a key element, signifies the Yin, the feminine energy. The fire, used to heat the water, is the Yang, the masculine energy. The tea brings these forces together and balances these struggling and competing energies.

The way of tea focuses on four basic principles that are believed to be essential to life. They are: harmony, respect, purity and tranquility. The tea ceremony is the vehicle through which these principles appear.

The ceremony is held in a tea house, which is a separate building in an outdoor garden. Before guests enter, the lush green garden is sprinkled with water to clear the dust from the outside world. Guests then pass through a gate and sometimes over a bridge that symbolizes leaving behind the harsh world of physicality and entering into the world of spirituality. Also in the garden is a stone basin containing fresh water. Guests ladle water over their hands and bring it to their mouths as a gesture of purification. The door to the actual tea house is only 36 inches high. All who enter must bow or pass through it on their knees, symbolizing humility and equality. For in the world of tea, as in the world of Spirit, all are equal.

Usually the tea gatherings involve two servings of matcha, which is a powdered green tea. The first serving, called koicha, is thick and rich, while the second, usacha, is a thinner version of the same tea. The usacha is drunk at the end of the ceremony to rinse the palate and prepare the guests for reentry into the physical world.

Although the Japanese tea ceremony is not as commonplace today as it was in the past, most Japanese have been taught the rituals, not so much as a course of study that must be completed within a given time frame, but as a tool for life. In learning to prepare tea with a pure and open heart, one can achieve self-mastery and inner peace.

Many other countries besides Japan have focused on the spiritual aspects of serving tea. When tea reached the European countries, however, the serving of tea became more of a social event. European high society, eager to impress their guests, began staging lavish afternoon gatherings, until "afternoon tea" became a social institution.

Is there a way to balance the social and spiritual aspects of tea time here in North America? A more relaxed atmosphere, a group of friends, soothing hot tea, and great stimulating conversation sounds like a wonderful way of tea. We have discussed how tea and quiet time alone does wonders for the mind, soul, body and heart. Now we may choose to open our homes and invite others in on this new way of tea.

We have already dealt with the clutter and disorganization of our homes in chapter two, so the prospect of inviting people over no longer has a daunting and overwhelming effect. A "lived-in" home puts most people at ease immediately; things do not have to be perfect.

The preparation need not be elaborate. We can prepare some simple but nourishing foods and focus on a nice presentation. This could also be a great time to bring out all those fine things that we have put away for that special occasion that never seems to present itself: Grandmother's china, Auntie's teapot, the vintage linens Mom made us take, those tiny forks we've never been sure what to do with. During the gathering, we can encourage thought-provoking conversation and focus on paying careful attention to the needs of each guest.

The new way of tea could be a perfect opportunity to purchase foods that are a little more exotic for serving to friends or family. The guests may be surprised, but it is always more fun to experiment with new things in the company of others. Whoever ate their first raw oyster all alone in their kitchen?

A tea ceremony is all about hospitality, creating new friendships and reestablishing old ones. How many times have we said or heard, "Let's get together soon?" But no one ever makes that call. An afternoon gathering for tea provides an ideal solution. No one expects a meal, so it's much less work than a luncheon or dinner party. With just a little imagination, you can dazzle your guests without days of preparation.

The host/hostess has one very important responsibility during a tea gathering. In this new way of tea, we want to be sure that the conversation remains positive and upbeat; any gossiping or griping defeats the whole purpose. We don't want to dishonour our gathering by allowing disparaging remarks or tiresome complaints to intrude. An attentive host or hostess can find a way to switch the topic of conversation, and guests will appreciate the effort.

The responsibility of the guests is to always R.S.V.P. to invitations with a *YES* or a *NO*.

Our homes are indeed where our hearts are, and when we open both, the world will be a kinder and gentler place. What a wonderful reason for creating a "new way of tea!"

Affirmation

My home is where my heart is.
My heart is in my home where all are welcome.

"Strange how a teapot can represent
at the same time, the comforts of solitude
and the pleasures of company."

~ Author Unknown ~

Equali-Tea

When God sees you, God sees me.
And in me God sees all there is.
So God sees God when God sees me.
When I see you, I can see me.
This is divine equality—where we are all in parity.
I accept the One, all parts of the One.
I can see the good in you and the good in me.
A divine equilibrium is keeping us in balance,
in perfect harmony;
all with the same power, potential and pedigree.
In the eyes of the Creator, all forces agree.
Thank you for allowing me to see through new eyes.
I release all thoughts of judgement and inequality.
There is no difference between you and me.
I open my heart, for love is the presence that always allows.
This is God's divine plan and love is the equalizer.
I stay quiet, I go within, and soon I am much wiser.
I am tolerant, kinder and gentler;
I am much more ME—the *me* that God knows me to be.
So I let that be and live in the harmony and symmetry
of divine equanimity with all of God's family.
Amen.

"Another novelty is the tea-party,
an extraordinary meal in that,
being offered to persons that have already dined well,
it supposes neither appetite nor thirst,
and has no object but distraction,
no basis but delicate enjoyment."

~ Jean-Anthelme Brillat-Savarin ~

Humani-Tea

As a people, as a collective, we are the human race.
No separation, no segregation—we each have a place.
We are all one with God. God is all there is.
Each and every one of us, children of God;
divine beings—being human.
Human beings seeking a divine experience.
For this experience I go within.
I am not just human, I am a humanist and I am humane.
Good and kind. Gentle and compassionate.
This is the real me, good as can be—a humanitarian.
I cause no suffering nor do I torment myself.
I embody and embrace all of humanity.
I accept God's diversity and creativity.
I thank God for my sisters and brothers.
For the perfection of myself and all others.
I see no division, only God's pure vision,
and the reality of eternity long beyond our humanity.
I release all human trifling and all past suffering.
I let go and let God's divine plan unfold for man.
And so it does.
Amen.

"Come and share a pot of tea; my home
is warm and my friendship's free."

~ Emily Barnes ~

Hospitali-Tea

There is a place in me of endless generosity.
I am open and giving, kind and friendly.
This is the *me* that God has always known.
From here, I know God is all there is.
We are one and love is all I am shown.
I accept this love and reject all else.
This love helps me project myself, my good,
my value and my virtue.
An open me extends love easily.
I welcome all others and socialize freely.
I open my heart and open my home,
and I see a whole new me –
confident, positive, living life, keeping it real.
I give thanks to God for the good I feel.
Giving is receiving for there will always be more.
Caring is sharing and will always open the door,
to who I really am and all I have to give.
I release all beliefs in a lesser me.
I let go and let God be, and I am
shown divine hospitality.
This I know, love I show,
and in God I grow.
Amen.

Affirmation

To know the unknown,
to show what is seldom shown,
I now claim for me.

Chapter Eleven

In Conclusion

Affirmation

I hold the key, I insert the key,
I turn the key, I unlock me.

In Conclusion

Along our way on this expedition into *Sereni-Tea:* **Seven Sips to BLISS** we have learned that we have "oodles and oodles" of choices. By breaking them down and implementing a few at a time, the process of healing, growing, loving ourselves, and finding our bliss becomes easier. No one wants to be overwhelmed, yet most of us have known many moments and sometimes many years, of feeling overcome by this "gift" of life.

We now know the power of our every thought—to make changes in our lives, our thoughts have to change—our thoughts about ourselves; first and foremost. To know peace is to stop thinking about hate and war. For prosperity, we release all thoughts of scarcity and lack. To love ourselves we must stop fighting ourselves—our own innate nature—for we are all born with the infinite ability to love.

Every thought we have creates our current reality and shapes our future—so every loving thought can do the same, with much more fulfilling results.

We have learned that we can elect to set aside time every day to reconnect and recharge ourselves; precious moments to settle the mind, and sacred seconds in communion with the soul. We can adopt a new way of praying and make prayer a part of our everyday lives. As we pray in celebration and gratitude for all we have, for all we are, and for all that we are capable of in God's light, we open ourselves to infinity and endless possibilities. All of this is loving the self—our God selves, as well as our human selves—the secret is to meld the two. *And this is how we learn to fall in love with ourselves.*

We have the option of a healthier lifestyle by making better food and beverage choices, one mouthful at a time. We can choose to take the dog for a walk in the fresh air instead of succumbing to the sofa and the television. We can also select tea, a simple, understated beverage to revitalize ourselves from the inside out. It is well-known that we certainly do celebrate with food and drink, but being "in celebration" of what we put into our bodies changes the energy and blesses what we consume. Loving the body starts in the mind, and a mind that has been turned over to God no longer has a need for overindulgences or harmful behaviours. Self-love also encompasses loving the physical body and by doing this, one is on the road to success and true bliss—a road travelled by few.

We can choose love above all else—love for ourselves and ultimately for all others. We can put love into everything we do, think and say. Celebrating love is affirming the infinite supply that we all have access to, a love for which our hearts are deeply longing. A heart full of love is a happy, healthy heart.

In our quest for success we simply must learn to forgive. For in forgiving, we open a door that otherwise remains locked. A door that is impassable blocks out all happiness, joy and bliss; without these we will never know self success. This door has to stay open, and so do we, for slamming it shut again will only serve to impede the wonderful feeling of wholeness and the blissful conscious connection with God—TRUE LOVE. And for those who we feel may have committed wrongs against us, and for those against whom we have trespassed, forgiveness has always been the key. It is the key that unlocks and unblocks us and allows us to open and expose all our God-given gifts. We do this for ourselves as well as for others, for this is also a gift, a gift that keeps on giving so that we can keep on living—living in the bliss of self success.

In this new space opened up by forgiving and loving and praying, we can choose to take quiet moments for meditation. A calm mind is a conscious mind through which God enters unrestricted into every aspect of our lives.

Karma teaches us that the power of divine right action and positive thinking will lead us down a new and fulfilling path. Choosing new thoughts and behaviours will surely lead us down a solid path, a safer path and a sacred path—this is the path to true bliss. There are laws and principles by which this universe of ours functions. The positive or negative thoughts we put out will determine what comes back to us. It is just that simple. So if life is tough right now, one must ask oneself, *is this what I have been drawing to myself?* The answer is *yes*. The tools for self transformation have been put forth in *Sereni-Tea:* **Seven Sips to** BLISS for those who are ready.

As we make ourselves available to love ourselves by releasing our *junk* and open up to new, and inspiring thoughts—the old, constricting thoughts will then release US. And in these moments of liberation, BLISS becomes possible.

When we rediscover our true LOVING selves, we will then know joy, and the self-destructive actions of the past will disappear. There will be no need for them any longer. The mind, body, soul and heart will all be in perfect alignment to receive love and guidance from higher sources. We have never been alone or abandoned, our *stuff* has just gotten in the way. Free of our restrictions, we become aware of the God presence in ourselves and in all others. This is when we know we are indeed all one with God, and that love is what unites us all—love for ourselves and for all others. This is indeed pure bliss and reason to celebrate our own success. Reason enough to take up the cup for fifteen minutes every day in celebration of both our Divine Self and our human self. Thus, we begin the process of falling in love with ourselves—and this is pure bliss.

Go ahead sip all you desire—you do deserve it.

"I am in no way interested in immortality,
but only in the taste of tea."

~ Lu Tung ~

Immortali-Tea

God is all there is, was, and will be.
The One lives eternally.
I am a spark from this Eternal Flame.
Our perpetual union is timeless and deathless.
I am one with the Forever-Living One.
God has given me everlasting life
and an endless appreciation for life.
I do not need fame to live forever—
just the Flame to live forever.
I can never be extinguished, I will shine
incessantly; always and in all ways.
Thank you God for being my torch—
my source of everlasting light and enduring goodness.
There is no darkness before me and none behind me,
and certainly, none within me.
I always choose the path that is lit with the light of love.
I am safe in the surrender
and warmth of this never-fading light.
I follow the light, and live by the light.
I am illumined and enlightened—forever.
Amen.

"One sip of this will bathe the drooping
spirits in delight, beyond the
bliss of dreams."

~ Milton ~

Adversi-Tea

I am no longer my own adversary.
I allow only good to flow through my life.
Perceived hardships and misfortunes
I no longer carry.
With my eyes open, God is all I see.
With my heart open, God is all I know.
I blame no one and forgive everyone.
No inflictions on me, no afflictions from me.
All these lessons I now can clearly see.
I accept them, and I respect them.
I now choose differently.
I elect to learn by doing good.
I embody the good within me,
and the good of the universe is all I see.
Loving God, loving life, there is no adversity.
The opposite is true prosperity.
In gratitude I live an adventurous
and prosperous life.
No more struggle, no fear, no strife.
God's vision becomes clear.
I see a new way;
I celebrate a new day.
I rest in this knowing,
and I keep on growing.
All is good, all is God,
and love keeps on flowing.
Amen.

"Tea, heaven's delight, and nature's truest wealth,
that pleasing physic, and pledge of health,
that statesman's counselor, that virgin's love,
the muse's nectar—the drink of love."

~ Peter Antoine Motteux ~

Certain-Tea

The infallibility of God is certain;
reliable and dependable,
a love beyond question.
This I know with indescribable surety.
In truth, God is all there is.
Something deep inside me knows that we are one.
A force beyond words,
an innate, inexpressible sureness,
assures me of an exceptional union.
I accept this extraordinary force of goodness
as a part of who I am.
I embody this aspect and
choose to exemplify this gift
as my contribution back to God's universe.
This I do out of gratitude,
with fortitude and in certitude.
I ask for no proof, for in God I am positive.
I give absolute thanks,
and in confidence and with conviction,
I release any dubiousness;
I relinquish all smallness.
For with God I grow and in God I know.
All else, I let go. And it is so.
Amen.

Affirmation

I've learned about tea,
I've seen the real me.
Loving me now comes easily.
So I let it all be.
And so it is and so I am free
from now, until eternity.
Amen.

Appendices

"We must be willing to let go of the life we planned so
as to have the life that is waiting for us."

~ JOSEPH CAMPBELL ~

Preparing the Perfect Pot

Begin by preheating the teapot with boiling water. For the actual tea, use good-quality water. If tap water is undesirable, use filtered or bottled water. Boil, but do not over boil the water; water with plenty of oxygen best releases the flavours of the tea leaves.

Fully boiled water is best for black and oolong teas. For white or green tea leaves, allow the water to sit for a few minutes after boiling or remove from heat just before it reaches the boiling point.

If your tap water is of good quality use only COLD water—never water from the hot water faucet. If you have ever replaced a hot-water heater then you will understand why. Water that is boiled in a microwave is not the same water anymore—do it the 'old-fashioned' way—in a kettle.

Pour out the water from teapot that was used to warm the pot. Measure one teaspoon of leaves per cup (hence the name "teaspoon") and add them to the pot. Pour the boiled water on top of the leaves. Allow to steep anywhere from 1 minute to 5 minutes, depending on the tea variety. In general, 2—3 minutes is fine for most varieties of tea. (Note: If you choose to use teabags, steep for even less time, since the leaves used in most bags are very fine.) Remove the leaves immediately if using an infuser, or catch the leaves with a strainer, or you can decant into another vessel before pouring the tea into the cups. Cover the pot with a tea cozy or use a tea-light stand with a lighted candle to keep hot for future cups.

White, green and oolong teas are best drunk clear. For black or flavoured teas, you may want to add lemon, milk, sugar, honey or other sweetener to taste. Sip slowly and enjoy completely. Some leaves, such as oolongs and many green teas, can be used again—the same day. Black teas are best used only once, although that is up to the individual.

Experiment with leaf amounts and steeping times. Drink tea the way you like it! Share a pot with a friend, neighbour or co-worker.

Chill remaining tea to use for iced tea, pour it into ice-cube trays to add to chilled tea, or sweeten and pour into molds with wooden sticks to create a fun and healthy frozen treat.

Glossary of Tea Terms

Agony of the leaves—in observing the leaf's "agony" (the process of the leaves unfurling) the quality of the tea's liquor can be predicted. This process reveals whether or not proper procedures were followed in the preparation of the leaves.

Afternoon Tea—a full service, mid-afternoon light meal, offering a variety of teas, small sandwiches and several fancy sweets.

Anhui—one of the major tea producing provinces in China.

Antioxidants—nutrients derived from certain plants, foods, vitamins, minerals and enzymes that help neutralize the effects of the oxidants or "free radicals." White and green teas are rich in antioxidants, but they are present in all teas.

Aroma—the characteristics of the fragrance of a fully steeped tea, derived from the natural essential oils in the leaves.

Artisan Teas—hand-sewn tea leaves that start as a ball or in other shapes and open in hot water to "blossom" or "flower." Can be full-leaf white, green or black tea leaves wrapped around a flower or group of flowers. These are very showy and appealing.

Assam—high-grade black teas grown in the state of Assam in northeast India, with a rich, strong, malty flavour, deep red colour, and great with milk.

Astringent—the dry taste left in the mouth after drinking teas.

Autumnal—tea produced and harvested late in the growing season.

Bergamot—an essential oil from the bergamot orange rind originally added to black teas, Earl Grey being the most famous, and is now blended in other tea varieties as well.

Black Tea—tea leaves that have been withered, spread to dry, crushed and oxidized fully to a brown colour, and sorted into grades. Most of the tea drunk in Europe and North America today is black tea.

Blend—teas of several types, or separate batches of tea combined for consistency of flavour, or for new flavours.

Bloom—a tea tasters' expression to describe sheen or luster present to the finished leaf.

Body—the fullness of properly grown, processed, stored and steeped tea.

Brick Tea—steamed and fully compressed tea leaves shaped into bricks for ease of transport and preservation. At one time, tea bricks were used as currency; today they are still available in very creative designs.

Broken—leaves that are processed through a cutter, or broken during handling thereby, reducing their size.

Caffeine—the stimulating compound found naturally in tea and originally called "theine." Amounts can be controlled by the steeping time—less steeping, less caffeine. Additionally, the more oxidized teas have more caffeine.

Catechins—a class of powerful, water-soluble polyphenols or antioxidants that are easily oxidized by the body, thus enhancing the immune system. Catechins are found in all teas.

Camellia sinensis—the botanical name for the subtropical evergreen plant from which all teas come.

Ceylon—the former name of Sri Lanka that now refers to the teas from that country.

Cha—the word for tea in Japanese.

Chai—a strong, spiced black tea usually mixed with milk and sugar, originating in India and known there as Masala.

Chamomile "tea"—one of the most popular herbal infusions, reputed to relieve stress, anxiety and indigestion.

Chest—a wooden container with an aluminum lining used for shipping tea.

Cream Tea—a term ordinarily used in tea rooms to refer to a small sampling of fruit and/or sweets served with tea.

CTC—a manufacturing term, short for "crush, tear and curl," for the process used with certain leaves to create stronger infusions.

Darjeeling—a region in the Himalayan foothills in northeast India famous for teas of exquisite bouquet, complex flavour and high astringency—commonly referred to as the "Champagne of Teas."

Dragon Well—a fine green tea grown in China with an herbal aroma and toasty flavour.

Dust—the smallest broken leaves left after processing, usually used in teabags for quick infusions.

Earl Grey—a black tea flavoured with bergamot oil and named for the British Prime Minister, Earl Grey, who was awarded the recipe from a Chinese diplomat in the early 19th century.

EGCG—(Epigallacatechin gallate) is the most powerful and most abundant of the four major catechins found in green tea. Antioxidants found in EGCG work to destroy free-radicals.

English Breakfast—a blend of several black teas, usually served at breakfast with milk and sugar for a gentle caffeine lift.

Estate—the property on which tea is grown; also known as a plantation.

Fair Trade—a certification qualification for the estate growing and processing the tea leaves; it ensures good quality-of-life standards for the workers.

Fannings—the tiniest particles sifted from good-quality grades primarily used in teabags.

Fermentation—the process of oxidation that takes place in the green tea leaves to create oolong or black teas.

Firing—rapidly heating the leaves to stop the oxidation process.

Flavonoids—a part of a group supplying the polyphenols (the antioxidants) found in teas. The most commonly referred to of this group are catechins.

Flavoured Teas—are any teas that have been scented and accented with spices, flavourings, and/or oils.

Flush—usually referring to the times of harvesting the young leaves, the first flush being in the early spring, and the second flush in late spring/early summer, with later flushes having stronger flavours.

Formosa—the island known today as Taiwan—where many oolong teas are produced.

Full—description of a strong, vibrant tea infusion.

Gaiwan Cup—a Chinese saucer, bowl and lid made of porcelain.

Gaiwan Service—with one hand all three pieces are held securely while the lid is adjusted enough to pour out the infusion leaving the tea leaves in the bowl.

Genmaicha—is Japanese green tea with toasted rice.

Gong Fu—(Gungfu) a style of steeping tea in China that involves short infusions repeated many times in a small pot.

Green Tea—lightly fermented or oxidized young leaves that are heated or steamed to halt the enzymes from breaking down, then rolled and dried; low in caffeine, light green in colour, bold vegetal taste, usually from China or Japan.

Gunpowder—young green tea leaves rolled tightly into small pellets that look like gunpowder and unfurl as they steep.

Gyokuro –a high-grade Japanese green tea grown in the shade; translates to "pearl dew."

High Tea—a late-afternoon meal traditionally served with meat and other dishes, commonly confused with "afternoon tea" but much less fancy.

Hojicha—a roasted Japanese green tea.

Jasmine—tea, usually green, scented with jasmine flowers. Higher-quality teas are rolled by hand into pearl-shaped balls usually referred to as "jasmine pearls."

Keemun—a fine grade of black tea from China with hand-rolled and twisted leaves. Highly aromatic and can usually be detected when blended with other teas.

Kenya Teas—a growing and expanding tea producing area of Africa that is a large exporter of black teas and uses no chemicals in the growing process.

Lapsang Souchong—a smoky-tasting black tea from China, where the leaves are placed over a fire of pinewood or pine needles.

Liquor—the term used to describe the water after the tea has steeped, referring to the colour and clarity. Sometimes is called the "cup" or the "infusion" also.

Matcha—a finely powdered green tea from Japan, used in their tea ceremonies, with a bright green liquor, slightly bitter taste and high in antioxidants.

Nilgiri—a black tea from southern India that flavours and blends well. The name refers to the mountain region of that area and the colour blue.

Nose—the aroma of the tea.

Oolong—a semi-oxidized, larger-leaf tea in-between green and black—stronger than green, smoother than black—extremely flavourful, highly aromatic, and may be rolled or twisted; directly translated means "Black Dragon."

Orange Pekoe—(pronounced "peck-oh") a grade of large, whole-leaf black tea specifying only size and has nothing to do with the flavour of orange.

Pan-Fired—leaves that have been steamed then rolled in iron pans or woks over a fire.

Pekoe—(peck-oh) a smaller, whole-leaf tea made from the youngest leaves and buds, which often have white hairs or a downy appearance.

Plucking—the process of harvesting by cutting the leaf from the growing bush, usually done by hand.

Polyphenols—the astringent compounds found in teas. They are a group of vegetable chemical substances shown to be strong antioxidants with potential health benefits. Higher amounts are found in white and green teas.

Pouchong—a scented, large-leaf tea, very light and floral, usually from Taiwan

Pu-erh—(poo-air) usually from the Yunnan province of southwest China. Damp green tea leaves that ferment microbiologically to a black leaf resulting in a very earthy and musty, but smooth-tasting tea. Usually aged and pressed into cakes.

Rolling—the crushing of the tea leaves to activate the enzymes to begin the oxidation process, after which the leaves appear to be curled when dry.

Rooibos—(roy-bus) a plant from the legume family which means "red bush" that is from South Africa; caffeine free, usually red but can be green, (when not roasted) very mellow, and can be blended with teas or other herbs, or flavoured.

Scented Tea—is any tea that is flavoured by the addition of essential oils, fruits and/or flowers.

Sencha—is Japan's most popular and widely drunk green tea.

Souchong—large-leaf teas plucked from the third and fourth leaves of the tea plant.

Tannin—an astringent substance that occurs naturally in some plants. Tea leaves provide a particularly high source. Because of their tannins, tea leaves steeped for long periods can result in a bitter taste unrelated to tannic acid polyphenols of other plants.

Theaflavins—the polyphenols from well-oxidized black teas that provide high antioxidant health benefits.

Theanine—an amino acid, unique to tea.

Theine—is a synonym for caffeine.

THÉ—the French term for tea.

TÉ—another term for tea.

Ti Kuan Yin—a very good quality, highly desirable and fragrant oolong tea from China, which varies in colour, has a strong and rich flavour, and translates to "Iron Goddess of Mercy."

Tippy—a term added to the grade of tea if, during harvesting, some of the top two leaves have a golden or white tip.

Tisane—(tea-zan) refers to an infusion made from the leaves, fruits or flowers of various plants.

White Tea—true white tea is an expensive tea that originally came from a rare variety of the Camillia sinensis. Now it refers to any young tea leaves or buds that are only withered (air dried.) When steeped, white tea has a very smooth and light, almost floral taste and is always delicate. White tea is believed to contain more antioxidants than any other tea. It has a soft, white downy appearance.

Withering—a process by which, after the fresh leaves are picked, sorted and weighed, the leaves are left to air dry, allowing the moisture content to be controlled before rolling and processing, thus preventing the breakage of the leaves.

Yixing—(ee-shing) the name of the Chinese pottery derived from a natural purple clay, from which unglazed and highly prized teapots are crafted. The teapots are excellent for black and oolong teas because they hold the heat for long periods of time. They are not recommended for white and green teas.

Yerba Maté—the Spanish name of a holly tree that grows in the forests of South America. Its leaves are made into a hot or cold beverage. Extracts of the plant are now being used in many dietary supplements for weight loss. It is a stimulant but often referred to as an herb. It is usually drunk from a hollowed-out gourd in trendy shops.

Yunnan—a province in southwest China that produces the majority of Chinese black tea and that is believed to be where the original wild tea plants grew.

The Tea Trilogy

Enjoy three inspirational books that will take you on a three-step process to finding your inner joy, and living with the inner peace BLISS will provide.

A TEA TRILOGY that takes you on a journey from the head, to the heart, to the Divine; while sipping tea. In the time it takes for seven sips of tea you can change your life; little by little, sip by sip, day after day, one thought at a time, and find your way to bliss.

Yes, we are a society that wants everything right now but there is great wisdom in slowing things down, praying, meditating, releasing and forgiving, loving yourself, and of course, for sipping tea. This is the ultimate intention of the Tea Trilogy—to take the time to love YOURSELF.

The book you are holding right now, **Sereni-Tea: *Seven Sips to BLISS***, will guide you to be at peace with your thoughts, to see life as the celebration it truly is through prayer, meditation, forgiveness, loving, and making empowered choices for your own well-being and serenity. Included are 36 healing and spiritual tea prayers.

Sancti-Tea: book two of the trilogy bridges the gap between the head and the heart. Once you are at peace with your thoughts the next growing step is to open your heart. It is said that the journey from the head to the heart is often the longest—it need not be. A peaceful mind will automatically make it easier to open the heart to heal and to love and be loved. This fiction, non-fiction combination adds an unusual twist to the world of tea and inner healing by taking the reader on 13 fictional journeys. It includes 60 healing and uplifting tea prayers.

Divini-Tea: the final step and the book that completes the journey of inner healing and self-discovery. What is next after you have made peace with your thoughts and healed your heart?—A relationship of your own with the Divine. A workbook of sorts that helps you analyze your previous relationship with what you believed God to be, what type of relationship you truly desire, and the space to make note of it. The same is done for praying and what past, current and desired results you hope for from praying. It includes 101 uplifting tea prayers to assist you on the journey of opening up to prayer and praying from a place of wholeness and oneness with the Divine.

Please enjoy them all with my best wishes and intentions for your serenity, bliss, peace of mind, and God connection.

Dharlene Marie Fahl

www.dharlene-marie.com

dharlenemarie@gmail.com

www.sensualiteas.com

I Am Tea

I am TEA;
almost as old as time.
I have shaped a part of ancient history.
Almost every country and culture knows me.
I have been more valuable than silver and gold.
Stories, legends and myths about me have been told.
I have traveled by ship, by camel, by horse and mule.
I was seen as priceless – as any exquisite jewel.
Put under lock and key – safe in a chest.
I was more special than the rest.
I am TEA.
Treasured and revered – presented to royalty.
Everyone wanted to sip of me.
The beginning of a revolution;
fighting because of me was never the solution.
Coveting me and hoarding me,
selling me and extorting me?
Using me to hurt others and benefit some?
All of this is not who I am.
I am TEA.
I am simplicity and tranquility.
I am but a humble leaf.
Drink of me – I offer you relief.
Sip me slowly – surrender away your cares and woes.
I am a neutralizer – with me there are no foes.
I have no enemy and neither do you.
I know all that you have been through.
How do I know?
I am TEA.
I am sincerity and clarity.
Look deeply into your cup; that is me you see.
When the cup is empty you will be full.
I give you all of my gifts;

my nutrients as well as my mysteries.
I have been sharing these for centuries.
Taking time with me is special time for you.
This I give you – this is all you have to do.
I am TEA.
I am vitality and longevity.
My treasures are free – drink the life out of me.
Locked tightly in my leaves are the secrets I keep.
Release me in water – allow me to steep.
Sip in solitude – drink of my fortitude.
I will share it with you – now you do the same.
Share me with others – don't even ask their name.
Respect and reverence for all in every sip.
I am TEA.
I am serenity and spirituality.
Drink me and you drink divinity.
Have a taste of unity and know we are all one;
all part of a grand design—a puzzle already done.
Each of us is a piece and offers their piece.
Drink tea, drink peace, drink equality.
See how easy and effortless it can all be.
All coming from a simple leaf like me.
I am TEA.

~ Dharlene Marie Fahl ~

Recommended Tea Resources

Most of the tea information used in this book has come from two reliable and highly reputable organizations; they are:

The Tea Association of the USA
Suite 825—420 Lexington Avenue
New York, NY 10170
Website address: www.teausa.org
E-Mail address: info@teausa.com
Mr. Joseph Simrany, President

The Tea Association of Canada
885 Don Mills Road, Suite 301
Toronto, Ontario M3C 1V9
Canada
Website address: www.tea.ca
E-Mail address: info@tea.ca
Ms. Louise Roberge, President

The **World Tea Expo** annually hosts a convention that brings the tea world together; i.e. tea vendors, tea blenders, tea shop owners, publishers, etc.

Contact: www.worldteaexpo.com.

For informative articles written by tea professionals from around the globe—www.tching.com

Afterword

Please allow me to introduce you to my friend and tea colleague,

Dan Robertson

THE TEA HOUSE / **World Tea Tours**

24125 W. 111th St. #400

Naperville, IL 60564 USA

Tel 630 961-0877 Fax 630 961-0817

Email: ddrteaman@aol.com

Dan Robertson is the founder and owner of The Tea House and World Tea Tours in Naperville, Illinois. He was born in New Haven, CT. USA, raised primarily in the Midwest and is a graduate of the College of Wooster, Ohio. He is a thirty-year practitioner and instructor of the martial art and health exercise Tai Ji Quan. Before venturing into the world of tea, in 1985 Dan established FRAMEWORK Video & Sound, a video production company specializing in documentary and educational programming. Although traveling to the orient previously, involved in the freight industry, it was his career as a filmmaker that took him to China in 1994 and again in 1995 to produce a documentary on tea. With two years of preparatory work he traveled extensively across China filming tea gardens, factories, teahouses, hospitals, universities, museums and historical sites interviewing tea experts in all areas. As an unexpected result, in 1995 he began his own tea business, drawing upon the resources and knowledge he had developed during his travels. Since then he returns to China nearly every year either to meet with suppliers, discover new teas, study or research. Since 1996 he has been organizing and leading the acclaimed China Tea Tour, where tea lovers from around the world get first hand experiences in tea making, history, culture and business. Now expanding beyond the Far East, he launched World Tea Tours in 2006 offering tours to tea producing and cultural areas around the globe. He is recognized as a pioneer in the field of tea tourism.

As an importer, wholesaler, blender and purveyor of premium teas and accessories, he is involved with many levels of the tea industry. He is a regular contributor to various tea trade periodicals, web blogs and tea news services and is a Contributing Editor for *TEA a Magazine*. Known for his informal and engaging style, Dan shares his passion for tea, lecturing around the world for businesses, educational and private groups. He has served as a regular presenter and speaker at the World Tea Expo and the Indian Tea Forum in India on tea ceremony, tea culture, tea industry and tea tourism. An authority on tea culture, history, production and trade, Dan conducts professional tea tastings classes and instructs courses in the Chinese tea ceremony. His DVD *The Art of Chinese Tea—The Tea Ceremony*, is a demonstration and tutorial on the gongfu style of tea making. His current project is the large format, panoramic photo book, *Cultures of Tea* which showcases the places and cultures that produce tea. He is also the founder and Director of the International Tea Cuppers Club www.teacuppers.com) a worldwide community of tea lovers, dealers and producers who taste and share their knowledge of fine teas.

The Tea House®—Importers, Blenders and Purveyors of the World's Finest Teas.

As in the Tang and Song Dynasties of ancient China, an appreciation of the subtle elegance of fine tea is experiencing a renaissance. Our objective is to promote the communion of body, mind and spirit, by expanding the knowledge of the way of tea and the appreciation of its consumption. Since 1995 it has been our pleasure to offer fine products from around the world. We enjoy sharing our passion for the best that the world of tea has to offer. We know that it can be a little confusing with so many wonderful products on the market today. We are honored by the trust our clients place in us and we work diligently to provide accurate and useful information about the items we offer. We select our fine teas from hundreds of samples sourced from dozens of tea producing areas. In many cases we travel directly to the gardens and factories to test them in person. All of them are wonderful on their own but many of these same teas are the ingredients for our blends. Our decision to offer a tea is carefully based on several parameters. Foremost are **quality** and overall **character**. Not only must a tea have the appropriate leaf appearance but the color, aroma and flavor characteristics should meet or exceed standards. **Uniqueness** is also a determining factor. We offer a number of teas which are unavailable to other buyers. In some cases, teas are made exclusively for us. **Rarity** is another quality. We do offer exceptional quality "popular" teas but we also enjoy introducing our clients to things they have never seen before. Certainly **value** is an important consideration and we do our best to acquire our products at the best price possible. **Authenticity** is also an important criterion. We know that just because a tea bears a famous name it does not mean that it comes from the authentic location also, even origin teas are not all created equal. We look forward to serving you and offering you an exceptional and memorable tea experience.

The Tea House products are available through fine tea business around the world, on our website www.theteahouse.com and in our Naperville, IL showroom 630 961-0877.

World Tea Tours® - The Leaders in Tea Adventure Travel

World Tea Tours is the original pioneer of tea adventure travel. Led by world renowned, professional tea authorities, the custom-crafted tours are a combination of abundant, hands-on, invaluable tea experiences mixed with real involvement with the native cultures of tea producing and consuming regions. Each unique tour offers unparalleled, educational experiences for the tea business professional and avid tea lover alike. World recognized experts in tea and tea tourism, the organizers of World Tea Tours were the first to lead commercial tours to China from North America, especially for tea. After extensive travel across China and Taiwan since 1989, the first official China Tea Tour took place in 1997. Since then, the scope of the programs has expanded to include many other countries. The name World Tea Tours was introduced in 2006. Tour members hail from all across the globe and from all aspects of the tea profession, as well as tea lovers. Regular tours include the China Tea Tour®, Tea Tour of India®, Tea Tour of Japan®, Ceylon Tea Tour® and the intensive Immersion Program® series. World Tea Tours also arranges private tours, customized to meet client objectives. Providing comprehensive experiences at exceptional value, all programs are created by tea lovers, for tea lovers.

More information on upcoming tours and programs is available at www.WorldTeaTours.com, via email at info@WorldTeaTours.com

International Tea Cuppers Club®

ITCC is a world-wide tea community of people who share

a passion not only for the finest teas but also for contributing to the refinement and evolution of the tea industry. Tea lovers, manufacturers, organizations, industry leaders, professionals, dealers, educators and consumers from around the globe, engage one another directly through innovative Cupping Events, Member Hosted Events, the Community Board and the **ITCC** newsletter. **ITCC** members have access to an extensive range of select, premium teas directly from the key production centers of the world, often in advance of them reaching foreign markets. Benefiting from their diverse origins and experience levels, Cuppers evaluate teas and provide feedback and valuable comments to producers and suppliers, influencing production and trends. In the quazi-virtual Cupping Events, members from all over the world are given a chance to register to participate in Cupping Events. Each Cupping Event focuses on specific teas or teas from certain areas. Limited to the first 16 registrants, participants (Cuppers) receive a Cupping Event Sample Kit which contains 2 ounce (57 gram) samples of usually 8 to 10 teas and other materials that help the Cupper to effectively evaluate the teas. The ITCC communicates the evaluations and comments back to the tea producers and suppliers for their use in efforts to advance production techniques and continue to create higher quality teas.

More information about the ITCC, Cupping Events and tea related news and issues, visit www.teacuppers.com, email info@ teacuppers.com or call 630 886-8060.

Cultures of Tea©

The simple green leaf of the Camellia Sinensis, is known by many names; Cha, Chai, Te, Tea, even Herbata. It is consumed by peoples of different cultures, all over the world and in as many ways as there are drinkers. "Tea" means something to nearly everyone yet that impression may be vastly different from one person to the next. For some it is a hot beverage that their Grandmother gave them when they had a cold. It may have been concocted with milk or sugar. For some it implies a clear, pale yellow infusion with fresh, grassy vapors drunk throughout the day. For others it is an ingredient in a mélange of spices, cooked together in milk and poured back and forth between larger cups to cool and froth. For others it is a refreshing, iced thirst quencher guzzled during hot weather, maybe with copious amounts of sugar. For still others it conjures images of small teapots and thimble sized cups from which are sipped liquors with the heady scent of flowers or suggestions of peach. Liquid gold. Perhaps it evokes sweet memories of affairs involving favorite porcelain cups and pots along with mouth watering pastries or savory morsels. Some think of it as a base to which they add different kinds of butters, grains, even salt. Perhaps it is churned in a wooden tube or even drunk on horseback. A few find it a reverent experience that nurtures the soul. Some like it strong while some enjoy it mild. Some prefer simple tastes while others delight in discovering myriad complexities. Hot, cold; clear, embellished; green, amber and countless variations. This is the culture of tea. And, to truly appreciate what tea is, one must have an experience, an understanding of the cultures that have produced it.

Cultures of Tea is a large format, photographic glimpse into the places and cultures that have been the source of tea for centuries, sometimes millennia. As man has carried it on his journey of evolution, tea has been shaped and modified but has also, in turn, influenced the very people who created it. In the extraordinarily vivid, panoramic pages of *Cultures of Tea*, the reader will find a portrayal of iconic landmarks associated with those cultures. Some are of tea itself; in tea gardens or estates, in various stages of process, implements that accompany tea or examples of its consumption. Mostly however, this work is intended to exhibit the magnificence and spirit of where it comes from.

For more information on Cultures of Tea visit www.culturesoftea.com

The Art of Chinese Tea —The Tea Ceremony

Educational and informative this DVD is a wealth of information on the Chinese Gongfu Tea Ceremony. Presented and performed by noted tea authority Dan Robertson, it includes a complete, narrated demonstration of a typical tea ceremony. Also included is a step-by-step tutorial so you may study at your own time and pace. There is also a section containing a slide shows on the history and evolution of the Chinese tea ceremony.

For more information on *The Art of Chinese Tea—The Tea Ceremony*, visit www.theteahouse.com or call 630 961-0877. Published by FRAMEWORK Video & Sound and Art of Engineering.

Wise Words Of Wisdom

"Life is a succession of moments. To live each one is to succeed."

~ Corita Kent ~

"How far you go in life depends on you being tender with the young; compassionate with the aged; sympathetic with the striving and tolerant of the weak and the strong; because someday in life you will have been all of these."

~George Washington Carver ~

"I have learned that if one advances confidently in the direction of his dreams, and endeavors to live the life he has imagined, he will meet with a success unexpected in common hours."

~ Henry David Thoreau ~

"Success consists of going from failure to failure without loss of enthusiasm."

~ Winston Churchill ~

"If you think you can, you can. And if you think you can't, you're right."

~ Henry Ford ~

"The person who tries to live alone will not succeed as a human being. His heart withers if it does not answer another heart. His mind shrinks away if he hears only the echoes of his own thoughts and finds no other inspiration."

~ Pearl S. Buck ~

"Many of life's failures are people who did not realize how close they were to success when they gave up."

~ Thomas Edison ~

"Six essential qualities that are the key to success: Sincerity, personal integrity, humility, courtesy, wisdom, charity."

~ William Menninger ~

"It is not the critic who counts, not the man who points out how the strong man stumbled, or where the doer of deeds could have done better. The credit belongs to the man who is actually in the arena, whose face is marred by dust and sweat and blood, who strives valiantly, who errs and comes short again and again, who knows the great enthusiasms, the great devotions, and spends himself in a worthy cause, who at best knows achievement and who at the worst if he fails at least fails while daring greatly so that his place shall never be with those cold and timid souls who know neither victory nor defeat."

~ Theodore Roosevelt ~

"Self-trust is the first secret of success. "

~ Ralph Waldo Emerson ~

"I've missed more than 9,000 shots in my career. I've lost almost 300 games. 26 times I've been trusted to take the game winning shot and missed. I've failed over and over and over again in my life and that is why I succeed."

~ Michael Jordon ~

"Would you like me to give you a formula for success? It's quite simple, really. Double your rate of failure. You are thinking of failure as the enemy of success. But it isn't at all. You can be discouraged by failure or you can learn from it, so go ahead and make mistakes. Make all you can. Because remember that's where you will find success."

~ Thomas J. Watson ~

"Success is a journey, not a destination."

~ Ben Sweetland ~

"Truth, self control, asceticism, generosity, non-injury, constancy in virtue — these are the means of success, not caste or family."

~ Mahabhara ~

"Every one of us, unconsciously, works out a personal philosophy of life, by which we are guided, inspired, and corrected, as time goes on. It is this philosophy by which we measure out our days, and by which we advertise to all about us the man, or woman, that we are. . . . It takes but a brief time to scent the life philosophy of anyone. It is defined in the conversation, in the look of the eye, and in the general mien of the person. It has no hiding place. It's like the perfume of the flower — unseen, but known almost instantly. It is the possession of the successful and the happy. And it can be greatly embellished by the absorption of ideas and experiences of the useful of this earth."

~ George Matthew ~

LIVING LIFE

"Normal day, let me be aware of the treasure you are. Let me learn from you, love you, bless you before you depart. Let me not pass you by in quest of some rare and perfect tomorrow. Let me hold you while I may, for it may not always be so. One day I shall dig my nails into the earth, or bury my face in the pillow, or stretch myself taut, or raise my hands to the sky, and want, more than all the world, your return."

~ Mary Jean Iron ~

"O, with what freshness, what solemnity and beauty, is each new day born; as if to say to sensate man, 'Behold! Thou hast one more chance! Strive for immortal glory!"

~ Harriet Beecher Stowe ~

"Anything you ask in this nature you have the right to expect and receive. But it is only as you let go of the lesser that you can take hold of the greater, only as you drop confusion that you can entertain peace, only as you transcend doubt and fear that you can be lifted up to the hilltops of the inner Life."

~ Ernest Holmes ~

"Don't ask yourself what the world needs; ask yourself what makes you come alive. And then go and do that. Because what the world needs are people who have come alive."

~ Harold Whitman ~

I will not die an unlived life. I will not live in fear of falling or catching fire. I choose to inhabit my days, to allow my living to open me, to make me less afraid, more accessible, to loosen my heart until it becomes a wing, a torch, a promise. I choose to risk my significance; to live so that which comes to me as seed goes to the next as blossom and that which comes to me as blossom, goes on as fruit."

~ Dawna Markova ~

"Meditate. Live purely. Be quiet. Do your work with mastery. Like the moon, come out from behind the clouds. Shine!"

~ Buddha ~

"When you were born, you cried and the world rejoiced. Live your life so that when you die, the world cries and you rejoice."

~ Cherokee Expression ~

"You must be the change you wish to see in the world."

~ Mahatma Gandhi ~

"There are only two ways to live your life. One is as though nothing is a miracle. The other is as if everything is."

~ Albert Einstein ~

"Carpe Diem! Rejoice while you are alive; enjoy the day; live life to the fullest; make the most of what you have. It is later than you think."

~ Horace ~

"The day will come when, after harnessing space, the winds, the tides, and gravitation, we shall harness for God the energies of love. And on that day, for the second time in the history of the world, we shall have discovered fire."

~ Pierre Teilhard de Chardin ~

"Life is an opportunity, benefit from it. Life is beauty, admire it. Life is bliss, taste it. Life is a dream, realize it. Life is a challenge, meet it. Life is a duty, complete it. Life is a game, play it. Life is a promise, fulfill it. Life is sorrow, overcome it. Life is a song, sing it. Life is a struggle, accept it. Life is a tragedy, confront it. Life is an adventure, dare it. Life is luck, make it. Life is too precious, do not destroy it. Life is life, fight for it."

~ Mother Teresa ~

"There is a time when a man distinguishes the idea of felicity from the idea of wealth; it is the beginning of wisdom."

~ Ralph Waldo Emerson ~

"Nothing can dislodge this inner and intuitive perception from our mentality; we know it as certainly as we know that we live. This is God in us knowing Himself. We are awakening to the realization that the Universe is perfect and complete. It gives. It is love. It is good and wills only good to all alike."

~ Ernest Holmes ~

CHI—THE LIFE FORCE

"To be sure, this requires effort and love, a careful cultivation of the spiritual life, and a watchful, honest, active oversight of all one's mental attitudes towards things and people. It is not to be learned by world-flight, running away from things, turning solitary and going apart from the world. Rather, one must learn an inner solitude, where or with whomsoever he may be. He must learn to penetrate things and find God there, to get a strong impression of God firmly fixed on his mind."

~ Meister Eckhart ~

"We are all bound to the throne of the Supreme Being by a flexible chain which restrains without enslaving us. The most wonderful aspect of the universal scheme of things is the action of free beings under divine guidance."

~ Joseph De Maistre ~

"He who lives in harmony with himself—lives in harmony with the universe."

~ Marcus Aurelius ~

"It costs so much to be a full human being that there are very few who have the enlightenment or the courage to pay the price. . . . One must abandon altogether the search for security and reach out to the risk of life with both arms. . . . One has to embrace the world like a lover . . ." ~ Morris L. West ~ "I firmly believe that all human beings have access to extraordinary energies and powers. Judging from accounts of mystical experience, heightened creativity, or exceptional performance by athletes and artists, we harbor a greater life than we know. There we go beyond those limited and limiting patterns of body, emotions, volition, and understanding that have been keeping us in dry-dock. Instead we become available to our capacity for a larger life in body, mind, and spirit. In this state we know great torrents of delight."

~ Dr. Jean Houston ~

"There is a God Power at the center of every man's being, a Presence that knows neither lack, limitation, nor fear, sickness, disquiet nor imperfection. This Presence and Power is at the center of all people and all things."

~ Ernest Holmes ~

"Life reveals itself to whoever is receptive to it. That we are living in a spiritual Universe, which includes the material or physical universe, has been the conclusion of the deepest thinkers of every age."

~ Ernest Holmes ~

"Life may have given everything to you but only that which you accept is yours to use."

~ Ernest Holmes ~

"When we remember that our aim is spiritual progress, we return to striving to be our best selves. This is how happiness is won."

~ Epictetus ~

"You are already a spiritual being. When the mind understands this and embodies its essence that which you are in the invisible will become more apparent in the visible."

~ Ernest Holmes ~

"Never depend on the admiration of others. There is no strength in it. Personal merit cannot be derived from an external source. It is not to be found in your personal associations, nor can it be found in the regard of other people, even people who love you will not necessarily agree with your ideas, understand you, or share your enthusiasms. Grow up! Who cares what other people think about you!"   ~ Epictetus ~

"The foundations of a person are not in matter but in spirit."

~ Ralph Waldo Emerson ~

"Spirit is an invisible force made visible in all life."

~ Maya Angelou ~

"Attach yourself to what is spiritually superior, regardless of what other people think or do. Hold to your true aspirations no matter what is going on around you."

~ Epictetus ~

CHOOSING TO CHOOSE

"We human beings do have some genuine freedom of choice, and therefore some effective control over our own destinies. I am not a determinist. But I also believe that the decisive choice is seldom the latest choice in the series. More often than not, it will turn out to be some choice made relatively far back in the past."

~ Arnold Toynbee ~

"We cannot live a choice-less life. Every day, every moment, every second, there is choice. If it were not so, we would not be individuals. We have the right to choose what we wish to experience."

~ Ernest Holmes ~

"It is not the level of prosperity that makes for happiness but the kinship of heart to heart, and the way we look at the world. Both attitudes are within our power. . . . A man is happy so long as he chooses to be happy, and no one can stop him."

~ Alexander Solzhenitsyn ~

"Through meditations, and by giving full attention to one thing at a time, we can learn to direct attention where we choose."

~ Eknath Easwaran ~

"And Joy is Everywhere; It is in the Earth's green covering of grass; In the blue serenity of the Sky; In the reckless exuberance of Spring; In the severe abstinence of gray Winter; In the Living flesh that animates our bodily frame; In the perfect poise of the Human figure, noble and upright; In Living; In the exercise of all our powers; In the acquisition of Knowledge; In fighting evils . . . Joy is there Everywhere."

~ Rabindranath Tagore ~

"To be always intending to make a new and better life but never to find time to set about it is as . . . to put off eating and drinking and sleeping from one day to the next until you're dead."

~ Og Mandino ~

"You are the way you are because that is what you believe about yourself."

~ Don Miguel Ruiz ~

"Happiness is when what you think, what you say, and what you are—are in harmony."

~ Mahatma Gandhi ~

PRAYER FOR THE MIND

"Lose all thoughts of discord and fear, and permit the true pattern to come to the surface. Remember that thought patterns are acquired; therefore, the mind that accepted them can reject them."

~ Ernest Holmes ~

"You get peace of mind not by thinking about it or imagining it, but by quieting and relaxing the restless mind."

~ Remez Sasson ~

"In prayer it is better to have a heart without words than words without a heart."

~ John Bunyan ~

"Faith is the power of prayer. Now what is faith? When you analyze faith you find that it is a mental attitude against which there is no longer any contradiction in the mind that entertains it."

~ Ernest Holmes ~

"Your nature is absolute peace. You are not the mind. Silence your mind through concentration and meditation, and you will discover the peace of the Spirit that you are, and have always been."

~ Remez Sasson ~

"Sometimes the most important thing in a whole day is the rest we take between two deep breaths or the turning inwards in prayer for five short minutes."

~ Etty Hillesum ~

"The secret of health for both mind, and body is not to mourn for the past, not to worry about the future, or not to anticipate troubles, but to live in the present moment wisely and earnestly."

~ Buddha ~

"A good mind possesses a kingdom."

~ Seneca ~

"The great mind knows the power of gentleness."

~ Robert Browning ~

"The energy of the mind is the essence of life."

~ Aristotle ~

"All the resources we need are in the mind."

~ Theodore Roosevelt ~

"A happy life consists of tranquility of mind."

~ Cicero ~

"A person without prayer is like a tree without roots."

~ Pope Pius XII ~

"Seven days without prayer makes one weak."

~ Allen E. Bartlett ~

"I have been driven many times to my knees by the overwhelming conviction that I had nowhere else to go."

~ Abraham Lincoln ~

"The greatest prayer is patience."

~ Buddha ~

MEDITATION FOR THE SOUL

"Still your mind in me, still yourself in me, and without a doubt you shall be united with me, Lord of Love, dwelling in your heart."

~ Bhagavad Gita ~

"Meditation brings wisdom; lack of meditation leaves ignorance. Know well what leads you forward and what holds you back, and choose the path that leads to wisdom."

~ Buddha ~

"Meditation is not a way to enlightenment nor is it a method of achieving anything at all. It is peace itself. It is the actualization of wisdom, the ultimate truth of the oneness of all things."

~ Dogen ~

"What lies behind us and that lies before us are tiny matters compared to what lies within us."

~ Ralph Waldo Emerson ~

"Say not, 'I have found the truth,' but rather, 'I have found a truth.' Say not, 'I have found the path of the soul.' Say rather, 'I have met the soul walking upon my path.' For the soul walks upon all paths. The soul walks not upon a line, neither does it grow like a reed. The soul unfolds itself, like a lotus of countless petals."

~ Kahlil Gibran ~

"Learn to relax. Your body is precious, as it houses your mind and your spirit. Inner peace begins with a relaxed body."

~ Norman Vincent Peale ~

"Your nature is absolute peace. You are not the mind. Silence your mind through concentration and meditation, and you will discover the peace of the Spirit that you are, and have always been."

~ Remez Sasson ~

"The soul is the one triumphant, indestructible, and unconquerable thing you possess."

~ Ernest Holmes ~

"What is soul? It's like electricity—we don't really know what it is, but it's a force that can light a room."

~ Ray Charles ~

"Neither a lofty degree of intelligence nor imagination nor both together go to the making of genius. Love, love, love, that is the soul of genius."

~ Wolfgang Amadeus Mozart ~

"In solitude be a multitude to oneself."

~ Tibullus ~

"Sometimes, simply by sitting, the soul collects wisdom."

~ Zen Proverb ~

"If there is light in the soul, there will be beauty in the person. If there is beauty in the person, there will be harmony in the house. If there is harmony in the house, there will be order in the nation. If there is order in the nation, there will be peace in the world."

~ Chinese Proverb ~

"Nowhere can man find a quieter or more untroubled retreat than in his own soul."

~ Marcus Aurelius ~

"Patient and regular practice is the whole secret of spiritual realization. Do not be in a hurry in spiritual life. Do your utmost, and leave the rest to God."

~ Swami Shivananda ~

"Enlightenment is your ego's biggest disappointment."

~ Yogananda ~

"The body is truly the garment of the soul, which has a living voice; for that reason it is fitting that the body, simultaneously with the soul, repeatedly sings praises to God through the voice."

~ Hildegard von Bingen ~

"Still, there is a calm, pure harmony, and music inside of me."

~ Vincent Van Gogh ~

"When we are unable to find tranquility within ourselves, it is useless to seek it elsewhere."

~ Francois de La Rochefoucauld ~

TEA FOR THE BODY

"Health is a large word. It embraces not the body only, but the mind and spirit as well . . . and not today's pain or pleasure alone, but the whole being and outlook of a man."

~ James H. West ~

"Know, then, whatever cheerful and serene, supports the mind, supports the body too."

~ John Armstrong ~

"Love does not only transform our mental and emotional nature, it also involves the physical system of our body which goes through profound changes as well."

~ David McArthur ~

"Evil does not naturally dwell in the world, in events, or in people. Evil is a by-product of forgetfulness, laziness, or distraction: it arises when we lose sight of our true aim in life."

~ Epictetus ~

"Health is a state of complete physical, mental and social well-being, and not merely the absence of disease or infirmity."

~ World Health Organization—1948 ~

"The body manifests what the mind harbors."

~ Jerry Augustine ~

"Relaxation means releasing all concern and tension and letting the natural order of life flow through one's being."

~ Donald Curtis ~

"Health, a light body, freedom from cravings, a glowing skin, sonorous voice, fragrance of body: these indicate progress in the practice of meditation."

~ Shvetashvatara Upanishad ~

"Health and cheerfulness naturally beget each other."

~ Joseph Addison ~

"We cannot expect to overeat or to eat the wrong things and have them agree with us. But there is an intelligence within us which will guide us into a proper diet . . . We cannot expect our food to agree with us if we are constantly condemning it."

~ Ernest Holmes ~

"Life is not merely to be alive, but to be well."

~ Marcus Valerius Martial ~

"I like a harmony of the whole body—likewise a certain harmony of the mind. As I grow older I can less easily get along without it."

~ Andre Gide ~

"Virtue, like health, is the harmony of the whole man."

~ Thomas Carlyle ~

LOVE FOR THE HEART

"The purpose of the heart is to know yourself and to be yourself, and yet, one with God."

~ Edgar Cayce ~

"When our eyes see our hands doing the work of our hearts, the circle of Creation is completed inside us; the doors of our souls fly open, and love steps forth to heal everything in sight."

~ Michael Bridge ~

"Your vision will become clear only when you look into your heart . . . Who looks outside, dreams. Who looks inside, awakens."

~ Carl Jung ~

"In our deepest moments of struggle, frustration, fear, and confusion, we are being called upon to reach in and touch our hearts. Then, we will know what to do, what to say, how to be. What is right is always in our deepest heart of hearts. It is from the deepest part of our hearts that we are capable of reaching out and touching another human being. It is, after all, one heart touching another heart."

~ Roberta Sage Hamilton ~

"You may not always be able to feel a deeper heart feeling right away, but stay focused in the heart. The sincerity of your effort can reconnect you to your heart current and start the juices flowing. To plug in, think of someone you love or remember what feels good, maybe a fulfilling experience. Feelings help you remember."

~ Sara Paddison ~

"The best and most beautiful things in the world cannot be seen or even touched. They must be felt with the heart."

~ Helen Keller ~

"The less you open your heart to others, the more your heart suffers."

~ Deepak Chopra ~

"Grown men can learn from very little children for the hearts of little children are pure. Therefore, the Great Spirit may show to them many things which older people miss."

~ Black Elk ~

"The essence of love, while elusive, pervades everything, fires the heart, stimulates the emotions, renews the soul and proclaims the Spirit."

~ Ernest Holmes ~

"By using your heart as a compass, you can see more clearly which direction to go to stop self-defeating behavior. If you take just one mental or emotional habit that really bothers or drains you and apply heart intelligence to it, you'll see a noticeable difference in your life."

~ Doc Childre and Howard Martin ~

"The only lasting beauty is the beauty of the heart."

~ Rumi ~

"Wheresoever you go, go with all your heart."

~ Confucius ~

"The thousand mysteries around us would not trouble us but interest us, if only we had cheerful, healthy hearts."

~ Nietzche ~

FORGIVENESS

"Doing an injury puts you below your enemy; revenging one makes you but even with him; forgiving it sets you above him."

~ Benjamin Franklin ~

"Lord, make me an instrument of thy peace. Where there is hatred, let me sow love. Where there is injury, pardon. Where there is doubt, faith. Where there is despair, hope. Where there is darkness, light. Where there is sadness, joy. O Divine Master, grant that I may not so much seek to be consoled as to console; to be understood, as to understand; to be loved, as to love; for it is in giving that we receive, it is in pardoning that we are pardoned, and it is in dying that we are born to eternal life."

~ St. Francis of Assisi ~

"He that cannot forgive others breaks the bridge over which he must pass himself; for every man has need to be forgiven."

~ Lord Herbert ~

"Anger makes you smaller, while forgiveness forces you to grow beyond what you were."

~ Cherie Carter-Scott ~

"The weak can never forgive. Forgiveness is the attribute of the strong."

~ Mahatma Gandhi ~

"The hatred you're carrying is a live coal in your heart—far more damaging to yourself than to them."

~ Lawana Blackwell ~

"The remarkable thing is that we really love our neighbor as ourselves, we do unto others as we do unto ourselves. We hate others when we hate ourselves. We are tolerant toward others when we tolerate ourselves. We forgive others when we forgive ourselves. We are prone to sacrifice others when we are ready to sacrifice ourselves."

~ Eric Hoffer ~

"Forgiveness is freeing up and putting to better use the energy once consumed by holding grudges, harboring resentments, and nursing unhealed wounds. It is rediscovering the strengths we always had and relocating our limitless capacity to understand and accept other people and ourselves."

~ Sidney and Suzanne Simon ~

"Not that we foster vice or place a premium upon wrong-doing, but that we understand the frailties of human nature and learn to overlook much. To him who loves much, much is forgiven."

~ Ernest Holmes ~

"Forgiveness does not always lead to a healed relationship. Some people are not capable of love, and it might be wise to let them go along with your anger. Wish them well, and let them go their way."

~ Real Life Preacher ~

"Nothing worth doing is completed in our lifetime. Therefore, we are saved by hope. Nothing true or beautiful or good makes complete sense in any immediate context of history. Therefore, we are saved by faith. Nothing we do, however virtuous, can be accomplished alone. Therefore, we are saved by love. No virtuous act is quite virtuous from the standpoint of our friend or foe as from our own. Therefore, we are saved by the final form of love, which is forgiveness."

~ Reinhold Niebuhr ~

"Home is where hearts open and forgiveness and acceptance are the rule."

~ Rob Kall ~

AGONY

"It may serve as a comfort to us, in all our calamities and afflictions, that he that loses anything and gets wisdom by it is a gainer by the loss."

~ Sir Roger L'Estrange ~

"Wisdom is nothing more than healed pain."

~ Robert E. Lee ~

"A wise man is he who does not grieve for the thing which he has not, but rejoices for those which he has."

~ Epictetus ~

"If you're going through hell—keep going."

~ Winston Churchill ~

"If you don't like something change it. If you can't change it, change the way you think about it."

~ Mary Engelbreit ~

"If we will be quiet and ready enough, we shall find compensation in every disappointment."

~ Henry David Thoreau ~

"It is not enough that one surrenders oneself. Surrender is to give oneself up to the original cause of one's being. Do not delude yourself by imagining such a source to be some God outside you. One's source is within oneself. Give yourself up to it. That means that you should seek the source and merge with it."

~ Ramana Maharshi ~

"The dark night of the soul comes just before revelation."

~ Joseph Campbell ~

"Defeat may serve as well as victory to shake the soul and let the glory out."

~ Edwin Markham ~

"Adversity is like a strong wind. It tears away from us all but the things that cannot be torn, so that we see ourselves as we really are."

~ Arthur Golden ~

"When it is dark enough, you can see the stars."

~ Ralph Waldo Emerson ~

"The art of living lies less in eliminating our troubles than in growing with them."

~ Bernard M. Baruch

"The best way out of a difficulty is through it."

~ Author Unknown ~

"I know God will not give me anything I can't handle. I just wish that He didn't trust me so much."

~ Mother Teresa ~

"There is in every true woman's heart, a spark of heavenly fire, which lies dormant in the broad daylight of prosperity, but which kindles up and beams and blazes in the dark hour of adversity."

~ Washington Irving ~

"Every difficulty in life presents us with an opportunity to turn inward and to invoke our own submerged inner resources. The trials we endure can and should introduce us to our strengths."

~ Epictetus ~

"Begin to live today as though you are an immortal being and all thought of death, all fear of change will slip from you. You will step out of the tomb of uncertainty into the light of eternal day. The night time of your soul will have passed and the eternal light of everlasting day will dawn as the great reality in your life."

~ Ernest Holmes ~

"Lord, inspire me with love, that I may teach sweetness. Give me patience, that I may teach discipline. Enlighten my understanding, that I may teach wisdom."

~ St. Augustine ~

"We should pour ourselves forth in greater love (whenever we begin to feel sorry for ourselves) and seek every possible avenue for expressing love, looking not to the results, but knowing all the while that love is its own healing."

~ Ernest Holmes ~

"Dear God, May every aspect of my being be converted to Truth. May every cell fall into place and serve a higher plan. I no longer wish to be who I was. I wish to be more. Amen."

~ Marianne Williamson ~

"Your whole life is a rehearsal for the moment you are in now."

~ Judith Malina ~

HUMANITY

"Nor would the ways of Karma be inscrutable were men to work in union and harmony, instead of disunion and strife."

~ Helena Petrova Blavatsky ~

"Pilgrimage to the place of the wise is to find escape from the flame of separateness."

~ Rumi ~

"We are each of us angels with only one wing and we can only fly by embracing one another."

~ Luciano de Crescenzo ~

"Do not believe in anything simply because you have heard it. Do not believe in anything simply because it is spoken and rumored by many. Do not believe in anything simply because it is found written in your religious books. Do not believe in anything merely on the authority of your teachers and elders. Do not believe in traditions because they have been handed down for many generations. But after observation and analysis, when you find that anything agrees with reason and is conducive to the good and benefit of one and all, then accept it, and live up to it."

~ Buddha ~

"When you examine the lives of the most influential people who have ever walked among us, you discover one thread that winds through them all. They have been aligned first with their spiritual nature and only then with their physical selves."

~ Albert Einstein ~

"Sometimes your joy is the source of your smile, but sometimes your smile can be the source of your joy."

~ Thich Nhat Hanh ~

"Responsibility does not only lay with the leaders of our countries or with those who have been appointed or elected to do a particular job. It lies with each of us individually. Peace, for example, starts within each one of us. When we have inner peace, we can be at peace with those around us."

~ The Dalai Lama ~

"We find greatest joy, not in getting, but in expressing what we are . . . Men do not really live for honors or for pay; their gladness is not the taking and holding, but in doing, the striving, the building, the living. It is a higher joy to teach than to be taught. It is good to get justice, but better to do it; fun to have things but more to make them. The happy man is he who lives the life of love, not for the honors it may bring, but for the life itself."

~ R.J. Baughan ~

"Ethical existence is the highest manifestation of spirituality."

~ Albert Schweizer ~

"Humanity finds itself in the midst of the world. In the midst of all other creations humanity is the most significant and yet the most dependent upon the others."

~ Hildegard von Bingen ~

"An individual has not started living until he can rise above the narrow confines of his individualistic concerns to the broader concerns of all humanity."

~ Martin Luther King, Jr. ~

"You must not lose faith in humanity. Humanity is an ocean; if a few drops of the ocean are dirty, the ocean does not become dirty."

~ Mohandas K. Gandhi ~

"A human being is a part of the whole, called by us, universe;

a part limited in time and space. He experiences himself, his thoughts and feelings as something separated from the rest, a kind of optical delusion of his consciousness. This delusion is a kind of prison for us, restricting us to our personal desires and to affection for a few persons nearest to us. Our task must be to free ourselves from this prison by widening our circle of compassion to embrace all living creatures and the whole of nature in its beauty."

~ Albert Einstein ~

"Humanity is never so beautiful as when praying for forgiveness, or else forgiving another."

~ Jean Richter ~

"Over the years I have developed a picture of what a human being living humanely is like. She is a person who understands, values and develops her body, finding it beautiful and useful; a person who is real and is willing to take risks, to be creative, to manifest competence, to change when the situation calls for it, and to find ways to accommodate to what is new and different, keeping that part of the old that is still of use and discarding what is not."

~ Virginia Satir ~

"There are no galley-slaves in the royal vessel of divine love— every man works his oar voluntarily!"

~ St. Francis De Sales.

"The possibility of stepping into a higher plane is quite real for everyone. It requires no force or effort or sacrifice. It involves little more than changing our ideas about what is normal."

~ Deepak Chopra ~

About the Author

Dharlene Marie Fahl is an entrepreneur and approaches everything she does with a universal, collaborative, and cooperative spirit. She is a CEO Space graduate and lifetime member.

She has been a retail gift shop owner, a healing centre owner and operator, a restaurant general manager, as well as a director of training for a restaurant company responsible for seven restaurants. Her education and training is in Hospitality Management.

Ms. Fahl is a certified tea specialist—certified by The Specialty Tea Institute of America. She has walked the tea fields in China and sipped tea in some of the finest tea shops in Beijing and Shanghai. She has also enjoyed a spectacular trip to the tea fields of Darjeeling, Dooras, Bhutan and Bihar in India. It is also her passion to visit tea shops across America and Canada. Dharlene Marie has also toured privately, The Charleston Tea Plantation in South Carolina, the first American tea plantation. She was in the inaugurating class (2008) of the American Tea Masters of America program in San Diego. Most recently, Ms. Fahl has visited the tea fields and factories in the breathtaking Shizuoka Prefecture of Japan, near the majestic foothills of Mt. Fugi.

Dharlene Marie was born in Saskatoon, Saskatchewan, Canada. She has lived in San Diego since 1990 where she currently resides with her two young-adult children. Maintaining her Canadian citizenship, the spirit of the maple leaf is ever present and alive in her although she loves Southern California.

She has been a member of Mark Victor Hansen's Inner Circle and trained and travelled with Mark for two years.

Dharlene Marie is passionately involved in writing romantic and spiritual poetry for the balancing of the masculine and feminine energies. Her poetry will be published this year and you can find her performing her poetry on stage in San Diego.

As an inspirational speaker, Ms. Fahl is available for book signings, tea demonstrations & tastings, tea & prayer meditations, slide shows of tea trips, private consultations for tea shops or any one-of-a-kind event with a best-selling author. She specializes in TEA TALKS & Tea Tastings in senior communities in Southern California and is willing to travel anywhere.

With true individual self success and personal bliss everyone wins; every company, every customer, and every community.

www.dharlene-marie.com dharlenemarie@gmail.com www. sensualiteas.com

Tea Talks

By Dharlene Marie Fahl

I take tea out into the community; however, I don't just 'talk' about tea in my TEA TALKS. I give all my groups a full-sensory experience.

Tea simply must be enjoyed with all the senses. Most people have never seen 'real' tea leaves; to see the dried leaves before and after making tea is quite a thrill for many. In Southern California we grow the Camellia japonica mostly as a decorative, shade-loving, winter-blooming bush. This shrub is from the same family as the tea plant, the Camellia sinensis. Both are from the Theaceae family or 'tea family.' One cannot make tea from the leaves of the Camellia japonica but varieties of the Camellia sinensis are what produce all the white tea, green tea, oolong tea, pu-erh tea, and black tea grown all over the world. I bring a small cutting from the Camellia japonica to my TEA TALKS; what is seen in my slide shows from trips to tea fields all over the world, is now in the hands of my sippers, as well. This will be as close as some will ever come to seeing a real tea plant.

Participants see the different dried leaves, the many colours of liquids from the infused leaves and smell all the different aromas from each tea variety. They touch the 'spent' leaves (the wet leaves) after they have been infused and witness what has transpired in the pot of water that provides them with the tea they are sipping and tasting while I tell them stories about tea and my tea journeys.

My true joy is presenting my TEA TALKS almost exclusively in senior communities. I can barely express the bliss I feel while sharing my tea demonstrations with these very receptive groups. It is indeed my pleasure to serve those that remain from our 'Greatest Generation.'

Please see my website www.dharlene-marie.com for details on the many styles of presentations I offer for groups large and small. I have conducted my TEA TALKS wearing a Japanese kimono, an Indian saree, in Chinese silk, and wearing pearls, gloves and fancy hats, as well. See the TEA TASTINGS & PRESENTATIONS page along with my EVENTS page on my website. I love TALKING about TEA—I have found my bliss and I am following it!

"We have had the privilege of having Dharlene Marie here, three times at our Center, for her fascinating TEA TALKS presentation on tea. Our seniors have greatly enjoyed learning about the history of tea, how it is processed, and then tasting the different flavors of teas from various regions of the world. It has been a fantastic and unusual learning experience and was very well attended." ~ Melinda Wynar, Program Coordinator North County Inland Older Adult Center, San Diego, CA

"I am the Activity Director at the Springs of El Cajon. I feel I was the lucky one when Dharlene Marie came into my Senior Community to present one of her TEA TALKS. My residents loved her and all the information she brought. What fun we had tasting the teas! We certainly are going to have her again because the word is out on what a great presentation she gave. I encourage everyone to have her come to your community. You will not regret it." ~ Cindy Boulanger, San Diego, CA

Take Time

Take time to think;
it is the source of all power.
Take time to read;
It is the fountain of wisdom.

Take time to play;
it is the source of perpetual youth.
Take time to be quiet;
it is the opportunity to seek God.

Take time to be aware;
it is the opportunity to help others.
Take time to love and be loved;
it is God's greatest gift.

Take time to laugh;
it is the music of the soul.
Take time to be friendly;
it is the road to happiness.

Take time to dream;
it is what the future is made of.
Take time to pray;
it is the greatest power on earth.

Take time to give;
it is too short a day to be selfish.
Take time to work;
it is the price of success.
There is a time for everything.

Author Unknown (Ecclesiastes 3:1-8) The Bible
Take time for YOU—you are a gift to the world—take time
with a cup of tea to love yourself. What you discover will
amaze you—and heal you—and it will move you right into
your power.

Transformation Media Books

Transformation Media Books is dedicated to publishing innovative works that nourish the body, mind and spirit, written by authors whose ideas and messages make a difference in the world.

www.TransformationMediaBooks.com • 866-326-7768

for more information, the latest titles or to purchase direct